*This is
Not the
End*

This is Not the End

EDITED BY
TABETHA
MARTIN

Foreword by
Paula Tusiani-Eng,
LMSW, M.DIV.

CONVERSATIONS ON

Borderline
Personality
Disorder

ALTHEA
PRESS

*This book is dedicated to
my beautiful sister, and the amazing
supporters and participants of the
BPD Awareness Page at
bpdawareness.org.*

Contents

Foreword

"All of this talk of Paula's wedding is getting to me but I don't know why. I guess I am a confused person. The world is turning and I am not." This is what Pamela, my 19-year-old younger sister, wrote in her diary on August 12, 1998, just 12 days after I became engaged.

Although she adored my fiancée and was genuinely happy about our wedding, on August 13, the very next day after her journal entry, Pamela cut her arm with a razor and had to be readmitted to the hospital. As my world was brimming with excitement, she was overcome by sadness and self-loathing—and she didn't understand why.

Six months earlier, Pamela suffered a major nervous breakdown while a junior at Loyola College in Baltimore, Maryland. Initially diagnosed with major depression after a brief psychiatric hospitalization, Pamela was released to her home in New York for outpatient treatment. It was during this period, in the spring of 1998, that previously unseen behaviors emerged—behaviors like cutting, self-mutilation, addiction, and suicide attempts.

At the time, it was extremely difficult to enjoy wedding preparations while my family was on a 24-hour crusade to keep Pamela safe from her negative thoughts. Expressing my joy—or even the slightest mention of the wedding—could mean extra trips to the hospital and added stress for my parents.

Although I did not widely share the details of Pamela's mental illness with others, I had a wonderful support system of friends, my fiancée, and family, which helped me get through this difficult time. Knowing how much my sister loved me, I wanted to be sensitive to the emotional pain she was in—pain greater than anything I had ever experienced.

The doctors eventually told us Pamela had borderline personality disorder (BPD), a diagnosis that finally made sense. It was as if the great mystery of Pamela's life had been solved. Impulsivity, fear of abandonment, intense personal relationships, and pervasive loneliness were long-held characteristics of Pamela's personality.

The doctors were hopeful that Pamela might get better with intense, long-term treatment. She lived in an open residential setting for 18 months in Massachusetts. It was there she discovered art therapy, poetry, and journaling as a means of expression, along with daily individual and family therapy. The setbacks always came, however, from her impulsivity.

After struggling with addiction and the trauma of a sexual assault, doctors suggested transferring Pamela to a closed dual-diagnosis residential treatment center in California, where they could treat both her depression and her substance abuse.

Pamela finally made great strides toward recovery in California. During those 11 months, she remained sober, found a part-time job, moved out on her own, had a steady boyfriend, drove her car, and lived successfully on a budget. More important, she learned to control her impulses. Despite all of her growth, however, she still suffered greatly from depression.

In a last-ditch effort Pamela's doctor put her on an MAOI antidepressant called Parnate—a mood-elevating drug that has certain food restrictions. Hard cheese was one of them. Although Pamela and her caregivers knew of these food restrictions, she was served pizza with cheese on it for lunch one day. Her blood pressure immediately spiked, causing a bleed in her brain. She was sent by ambulance to a hospital, where the ER doctor treated her like a delirious mental health patient with a history of drug abuse instead of focusing on her medical symptoms, ordering a CT scan, and giving her life-saving, blood pressure–lowering medication. Tragically, Pamela died three days later, on April 19, 2001.

With the settlement from the malpractice lawsuit against the residential facility and hospital where Pamela was treated, our family founded the Borderline Personality Resource Center at New York–Presbyterian Hospital in White Plains, New York. The center's mission is to provide a call-in service for patients and families seeking treatment resources for BPD, and to raise awareness about the disorder. Since 2003, the center has served over one million individuals through its website, videos, and referral service.

Throughout her entire three-year struggle, Pamela kept copious diaries. It wasn't until 2009 that my mother and I took these diaries and placed them in counterpoint to our own family experience to tell Pamela's story in *Remnants of a Life on Paper: A Mother and Daughter's Struggle with Borderline Personality Disorder*. My wedding, and how it affected Pamela and our family, was part of that narrative.

I was married on August 1, 1999, and it turned out to be one of the happiest days of my life. My sister was my maid of honor. Although she is no longer with us, I have wonderful memories of her dancing at my wedding, intensely happy, with a wide smile that I will never forget.

However, Pamela's diaries reveal how hard it was for her to walk down the aisle and make it through the reception. She was incredibly anxious—nervous about pleasing me, as well as managing other people's not-so-subtle stares. Looking back, I wish I had been more compassionate toward her by validating her concerns, and by not placing unrealistic expectations on her or judging her appearance or actions. But I know more about BPD now than I did then.

Despite any lingering regrets, Pamela was always so much more than her diagnosis. She was a bright, fun-loving, extremely creative, artistic woman. She cared so much about others and had a mature capacity to reflect about her own experiences. I hope people remember her for those wonderful parts of her personality.

In fact, when my children now flip through my wedding photo album, and ask, "Was that your sister, Aunt Pamela?" I say, "Yes! Isn't she beautiful? Did you know that she loved to paint and dance?" And their eyes twinkle with the same love and admiration I have for her.

My hope is that through *Remnants of a Life on Paper* and projects like *Borderline Personality Disorder: New Perspectives on Recognizing, Understanding, and Recovering from BPD* we can create more empathy and understanding for people who are living with BPD. By raising awareness about BPD and speaking out about the need for more accessible treatments, those affected by BPD will both survive and thrive, well beyond the 23 years Pamela spent on this earth.

PAULA TUSIANI-ENG, LMSW, M.DIV.,
Garden City, New York

Introduction

Symptoms of borderline personality disorder (BPD) were first described as early as three thousand years ago, though it wasn't until the mid-1900s that the disorder gained notice and research on it began. Patients with BPD were seen as untreatable, and many seeking assistance were turned away. Due to technological advances like brain imaging, biochemical testing, and genetic testing, it is now known that there are biological influences and contributors to BPD: There is a real medical basis for the disorder. People with BPD are not "seeking attention," as so many suggested prior to scientific studies. These are real people with *real* struggles—people who need patience, understanding, and love.

Imagine a young man who is known for being outgoing, loud, and uninhibited. He likes fast cars and loves to party. He may come from a seemingly loving and supportive family, making it hard for many to understand his actions. Some view him as "spoiled;" others see such behavior as "attention seeking." His siblings are "healthy," popular,

In simple terms, people with BPD simply react without forethought or premeditation.

and do well in school. Most people assume it's just a phase—this can't be anything serious.

But it may be more than a phase. Brain imaging has shown that people with BPD have an opposing reaction in the prefrontal cortex of the brain compared to a "neurotypical" subject (someone without any major deviation from "normal"). The prefrontal cortex is known as the personality area of the brain and is responsible for decision making, personality expressions, social behavior control, and complex cognitive behavior. The latter is the executive function, where thought differentiation occurs. It's what allows a person to decide whether something is good or bad, determine future implications of present actions, make plans, and set goals. While many people view those with BPD as dishonest or manipulative, brain scans suggest otherwise: Data shows that the prefrontal cortex shuts down when those with BPD become stressed, therefore preventing them from purposefully lying or manipulating. In simple terms, people with BPD simply react without forethought or premeditation.

Studies have shown those with BPD have hypothalamic-pituitary-adrenal axis dysregulation and in a more recent discovery, lack of oxytocin. In lay terms, this means individuals with BPD show an increased biological stress response compared to those without BPD. Studies show that when introduced to a stressful situation, those suffering from BPD have an initial high rate of cortisol, i.e., stress. This implies, simply, that their body is *always* stressed. When these individuals are exposed to a stressful situation, they experience a delayed response of stress hormones, which are already in a heightened state. Afterward, when removed from the stressful situation, a neurotypical individual will experience recovery from the stressful event, whereas those with BPD actually have a heightened and prolonged recovery from stress. Imagine walking around in a constant high-stress state. Now imagine already being stressed, and probably anxious as a result, having an interaction that you perceive as upsetting with someone. Your body is already in fight-or-flight mode. How do you think you might feel or react? Would you lash out? Would you say things you might not otherwise say?

Reconsider the young man you imagined previously. His outgoing behavior and loud personality certainly don't make you think he has anxiety in social situations. Ask yourself: Could this behavior be a mask? Is it his way of hiding insecurities, even from himself? If he can't trust, then why would he go from relationship to relationship, knowing he continues to always have the same issues? People struggling with BPD *want* to trust; they want to find deep and meaningful love. But those with BPD fear rejection and abandonment, leading many to end, leave, or sabotage a relationship in order to feel like they are in control and to avoid feelings of rejection.

One of the biggest stigmas in the mental health field is labeling people according to their diagnosis. "That borderline . . . ," or "I'm borderline," are seemingly innocent ways to identify an individual or describe one's self. However, a person's mental illness doesn't define that individual. BPD should not be a label, nor should it be a defining characteristic. They are individuals *with* BPD. It does *not* have *them*.

While there are many helpful resources and books available to learn about BPD, associated treatments, and how loved ones can better interact with and support their loved one with BPD, this book takes a different approach. In this book, we offer you a chance to see inside the lives of those affected by BPD. You will read stories from individuals who have struggled with the disorder, as well as stories from loved ones and professionals living and working with those affected by what can be a confusing and frustrating disorder. The essays within provide a range of experiences surrounding BPD; it is our hope they will give you some insight. All opinions given by the contributors are their own, and this book is not suggesting readers follow any of the advice given. This book should be used as a tool to further self-exploration and a deeper understanding of the disorder, and any concerns, for either yourself or a loved one, should be addressed to a qualified mental health professional.

If you are someone struggling with BPD, we hope you will find courage and guidance. If you are someone with a loved one with BPD, we strive to give you understanding and confidence that there is recovery. Finally, if you are a professional, hopefully you will learn what life is like for those with BPD and their loved ones, and how to better approach your future patients.

These essays were written by individuals who have struggled with BPD and have sought help, as well as those who have walked side-by-side with their loved ones struggling with the disorder. You'll hear from folks with many different backgrounds and locales—as well as a variety of paths to diagnosis. You may identify with some or all of them. Hopefully, reading the following pages will widen your awareness about just how diverse this population can be.

PART I

UNDERSTANDING BORDERLINE PERSONALITY DISORDER

Despite being a well-established diagnosis for decades, BPD has only recently gained enough of a spotlight in the mental health community to receive proper research into its cause and treatment options. By better understanding that BPD works as an "emotional regulation disorder" and not through chemical imbalance, many in the field have worked to alter or even create therapies specific to patients suffering with BPD. Here we will take a brief look at BPD, its causes, and the research-supported therapy options available today.

An In-Depth Look at BPD

BPD and its symptomology were first described in a 1938 article written by Adolf Stern, "Psychoanalytic Investigation of and Therapy in the Borderline Group of Neuroses" in 1938, and published in *The Psychoanalytic Quarterly*. Most of the symptoms listed created the diagnostic criteria still used today. Stern referred to this group of symptoms and the individuals suffering from them as "the border line group." He used this term to describe the apparent overlap of symptoms of schizophrenia and nonschizophrenic psychoses, along with conditions such as anxiety and depression.

Many professionals saw this diagnosis as only useful for those who did not fit another diagnosis and would not respond to treatment. The term *borderline personality disorder* eventually appeared in the third edition of the *Diagnostic and Statistical Manual of Mental Disorders*, in 1980. Within the following 10 years, research showed that medication was indeed helpful in some cases, and scientific evidence showed biological disturbances were evident in those with BPD.

Identifying BPD

The current *Diagnostic and Statistical Manual of Mental Disorders*—the *DSM-5*—requires that five of the following nine traits be exhibited in an individual for the diagnosis to be met:

FRANTIC EFFORTS TO AVOID REAL OR PERCEIVED ABANDONMENT

An undercurrent of fears of abandonment often leads individuals who struggle with BPD to perceive a threat even in unthreatening scenarios and interactions. For example, an otherwise innocuous comment from a loved one or colleague might be taken as snide or curt. This sort of perception not only affects close relationships, but also a person's self-esteem and behavior. When people feel they are easily abandoned, their self-worth is in jeopardy, which sometimes makes them feel as though there is nothing good about them—nothing that others want to be around. This can lead to a depressive mentality. When fear of abandonment is triggered, people struggling with BPD may push away individuals who are close to them, or cling to those individuals in an unhealthy manner. Individuals may also turn to self-destructive or self-harming behaviors as ways to cope with feelings of rejection.

A PATTERN OF UNSTABLE AND INTENSE INTERPERSONAL RELATIONSHIPS

Individuals who struggle with BPD find interpersonal relationships difficult to maintain. They often experience idealization or devaluation, known as "black-and-white thinking," in relation to those close to them—not only in romantic relationships, but with family and friends as well. This behavior is one of the most defined, marked traits of those who struggle with BPD.

IDENTITY DISTURBANCE

Having a sense of self is important to understanding who you are. People with BPD can and often do struggle with a clear self-image. Frequent employment changes, trying different lifestyles, and even taking up and frequently changing hobbies can all be expressions of this struggle.

IMPULSIVITY THAT CAN BE SELF-DAMAGING

Self-damaging impulsivity can include (but is not limited to) risky sexual relationships and behaviors, financial irresponsibility, substance abuse, eating disorders, other forms of physical self-harm, and even reckless driving. Impulsive behaviors can be a mechanism for individuals with BPD to cope with emotions—and may or may not be noticed by those around them.

Sexual behaviors can be self-harming when they put close relationships in jeopardy or endanger the person physically or emotionally. Engaging in risky sexual practices can have a dangerous outcome on one's physical and emotional well-being. Impulsivity in finances relates to unchecked spending, often leaving the sufferer without the funds needed for basic necessities.

Eating disorders often accompany those with BPD. Eating habits can range from anorexia as a form of self-punishment when feeling shame or guilt, to binge eating for the same reasons, to feeling happy and carefree in the moment and not leveling current actions with long-term effects.

SUICIDAL THOUGHTS

Thoughts of suicide can consume those struggling with BPD, often materializing in the form of self-harm, dangerous behaviors, or threats of suicide. A very large percentage of those struggling with BPD suffer from suicidal thoughts, and many people actually attempt to take their own life. In fact, suicide is the leading cause of death in those who suffer from BPD. Over 75 percent of patients with BPD attempt suicide—some more than once. One in 10 people with BPD who attempt suicide succeed in killing themselves.

AFFECT INSTABILITY

In psychology, the term *affect* is used to describe emotion or feeling. Individuals suffering from BPD experience not only intense feelings and emotions, but also extremely reactive moods. They might feel a range of emotions, from euphoria to anxiety to irritability, all within a short period of time. While people free from BPD typically experience all of these emotions, the difference here is how quickly people with BPD can shift. Sometimes, all of these emotions will cycle through a person with BPD within an hour, or even faster. Often, individuals will keep cycling as they struggle to cope and understand their feelings until they find an outlet—often an impulsive or self-harming behavior.

FEELINGS OF EMPTINESS

Many of those with BPD struggle with feelings of emptiness. To avoid these feelings, they often seek company of others. Some move quickly from one romantic relationship to another, perhaps in hope of filling a perceived void. Others never want to be alone and always have a friend near, on the phone, or online. Doing so can help fill the void of emptiness, at least for a little while.

INAPPROPRIATE, INTENSE ANGER

It's been shown that people with BPD are constantly in fight-or-flight mode, always looking for threats. Being both reactive to the environment *and* sensitive to those around them, individuals with BPD can experience overwhelming feelings—feelings that can result in intense and inappropriate anger.

Imagine coming home from a long day at work. You feel like you didn't get anything important done and are worried about how your boss sees you. You walk in the door and your family member starts talking to you about everything that needs to be done at home, everything that hasn't been done, and plans for the coming weekend. Seems like a pretty normal day for many, right?

When people with BPD feel unproductive, they genuinely feel useless. They worry they will be fired and feel as if they are not good enough for anything. Walking in the door, they are *severely* stressed and anxious—maybe even depressed. Hearing things that haven't been accomplished or what they need to get done at home, they feel overwhelmed and ambushed, they may not perceive that they are simply being communicated with or that their partner is trying to engage them. They feel hate and anger toward whoever is making them feel more overwhelmed than they already were; they may even feel attacked. Suddenly, they are yelling, throwing things, and slamming doors. Immediately after, many feel guilt and shame at their reaction, knowing that their family member was just trying to talk with them, rather than make them feel unproductive or even more useless.

TRANSIENT PARANOIA OR DISSOCIATIVE SYMPTOMS

When presented with a stressful situation or environment—an environment in which people with BPD cannot resolve their feelings—individuals with BPD may disassociate or experience para-noia. Paranoia often presents as hearing voices or perceiving reactions from others that aren't there, particularly in times of stress and depres-sion. These voices often talk down to the individuals, telling them they are useless, annoying, worthless, and should harm themselves or others. Disassociation—feeling disconnected from one's own thoughts or sense of self—often stems from feeling deep pain and is used as a way to cope with current environments or experiences.

> Which of the above traits do you identify with?
> Which do you struggle with the most?

Types of BPD

With nine symptoms described in the *DSM-5*, there are theoretically 256 possible combinations and presentations of BPD. Many patients present with more than five symptoms—and sometimes all of them. That being said, in his 1995 book, *Disorders of Personality: DSM-IV and Beyond*, Theodore Millon identified four types of BPD.

DISCOURAGED BPD

In discouraged BPD, behavior will appear clingy and often subdued (depressive and restrained), with individuals never wanting to ven-ture too far outside of their comfort zone. They hide anger and are prone to explosive outbursts once they finally "have had enough." Patients with this type of BPD often self-harm and are suicidal, turning their emotions inward rather than lashing out at others. Sometimes, individuals with BPD may be incredibly attached to one or both parents, or a friend (not necessarily a romantic partner).

They view these individuals as their world. Any attempt to encourage independence and individuality is seen as a terrible rejection.

IMPULSIVE BPD

Individuals with impulsive BPD are often known as the life of the party. *Impulsive* is a word that describes them well, as they are often captivating, flirtatious, and energetic. They do not think before they act, and often cause chaos in their own lives, as well as the lives of those around them. They will go to extreme lengths to gain approval, receive attention, and avoid abandonment.

PETULANT BPD

Patients with petulant BPD are unpredictable and irritable. They are pessimistic and untrusting. They want to rely on others, but fear being let down. They are often resentful and stubborn, and struggle with feelings of worthlessness. Again, their anger is often very explosive. Many would describe individuals with petulant BPD as passive-aggressive and controlling, using their behaviors to avoid abandonment.

SELF-DESTRUCTIVE BPD

Bitter would be a good word to sum up individuals with self-destructive BPD. They are self-destructive, whether or not they are conscious of their behavior, and are often lacking self-care skills and prone to participating in humiliating, degrading acts. This category of patients with BPD is often very challenging, even for the most qualified and experienced professional. Many identify this type of BPD as the "classic cultural image" of BPD. They feel like no one cares about them, and, as a result, they do not care for themselves.

Coexisting Conditions

Many individuals struggling with BPD also struggle with co-occurring disorders. Sometimes, these conditions happen alongside BPD; other times, they occur as a result of BPD. The most common comorbid disorders are described next.

DEPRESSION
Depression is believed to exist in at least 70 percent of patients with BPD, and many professionals believe depression occurs universally in all patients suffering with BPD.

SUBSTANCE ABUSE
Substance abuse, occurring in about 35 percent of those with BPD, can come in many forms. Often, it is a way for those suffering with BPD to cope with emotions or address their own undesired behaviors. This behavior must be treated prior to treatment for BPD. Once substance abuse is under control, treatment for BPD must begin, or relapses of abuse will likely occur.

EATING DISORDERS
Eating disorders occur in about 25 to 30 percent of patients with BPD. It is considered a means of self-harm, in addition to meeting a desire to feel in control. A high percentage of individuals with BPD are specifically affected by bulimia.

NARCISSISTIC PERSONALITY DISORDER
Narcissistic personality disorder co-occurs in about 25 percent of individuals with BPD. This personality disorder encompasses a need for admiration, an inflated sense of self, a lack of empathy for others,

and an extremely fragile and vulnerable self-esteem. Like BPD, this disorder affects interpersonal relationships, financial stability, and employment.

BIPOLAR DISORDER

BPD and bipolar disorder are often confused for one another. While they may have similar traits, the former is a personality disorder while the latter is a mood disorder. Bipolar disorder is characterized by mood swings between mania and major depression, sometimes lasting weeks at a time. The mood swings of BPD, however, encompass a whole host of emotions, including fear, depression, anxiety, happiness, and anger. For a BPD patient, these moods can do a complete cycle in minutes, rarely lasting more than a few hours.

Several of the contributors in this book also struggle with these coexisting conditions. Do any of them resonate with you, either personally or with a loved one?

The Four Phases of Treatment

Harold Searles became one of the pioneers in treating BPD. In his book, *My Work with Borderline Patients*, he delves into expanding his psychodynamic, four-phase, object-relation approach to those with BPD. This four-phase approach is an outline of what to expect in therapy progression, with the knowledge that each person's treatment will look different. Sometimes patients will experience phases overlapping, and sometimes they may revert to a previous stage. It can be argued that the four stages of dialectical behavioral therapy (DBT) are reflective of the following four stages.

OUT-OF-CONTACT PHASE

Presenting patients will often experience an extreme disconnect from the world around them, frequently in the form of dissociation and hopelessness. Their newfound relationship with their therapist is foreign to them. Daily functioning and life skills can be severely impaired.

AMBIVALENT SYMBIOSIS PHASE

Through treatment, patients begin to experience hope for recovery. At this time, they long to repair and rebuild existing relationships and make new ones. They will attempt to trust their therapist, though some will still act withdrawn and fearful. The patient may be able to now approach employment and relationships in a more consistent manner, but may still be very fragile.

THERAPEUTIC SYMBIOSIS PHASE

The therapeutic symbiosis phase begins when trust between the therapist and patient has been built and is strong. Here, Searles views the therapist in a nurturing role for their patient. It is important to note that this phase should be prolonged to allow for full growth and healing. This phase is also when patients with BPD begin to experience and recognize a sense of self-identity—something they have spent a lifetime struggling with. Here, they will experience more rewarding work and relational experiences, without the fear of separation and loneliness.

RESOLUTION OF THE SYMBIOSIS PHASE

The resolution phase marks an increase in self-awareness and concrete self-identity. Therapists are now seen as a separate entity and the frequency of sessions gradually decreases. Patients are now able to resolve conflict in their lives on their own.

Therapeutic Interventions

While psychotherapy was the first therapy to be used for those with personality disorders, its unsatisfying success rate led to the development of better, more effective treatments. The following are the current leading therapies recognized, via peer-reviewed research, by the psychology field today.

DIALECTICAL BEHAVIOR THERAPY

Marsha Linehan, PhD, created dialectical behavioral therapy (DBT), which specifically focuses on emotional regulation. As someone who had struggled with BPD, Linehan designed the therapy after her own experience of healing. It was originally designed to treat patients with reoccurring suicidal ideation. DBT utilizes different therapy approaches and settings, including individual and group sessions. Compared to the high rate of patients with BPD dropping out of traditional therapy, DBT patients are twice as likely to stay in therapy. The DBT treatment model consists of four stages:

1. **Regain control.** The patient may self-harm, or be self-destructive or even suicidal. In this stage, the goal is to move patients from being out of control of their behaviors to being in control.
2. **Address lack of emotional release.** With behavior under control, patients now experience frustration at a lack of emotional release. Their emotions are often muted. The goal becomes moving patients into full emotional experiences.
3. **Develop self-esteem and goals.** Here, patients will work on self-esteem and defining goals for their life. Happiness and peace are the hopeful outcomes of this stage.

4. **Work toward fulfillment.** The final stage is designed for those who need or want spiritual fulfillment in life. The goal of this stage is for patients to experience a feeling of wholeness, joy, and freedom.

COGNITIVE THERAPY

Aaron Beck, MD, developed cognitive therapy in the 1960s. In this approach, patients are seen as having a dysfunctional view of themselves and others. The goal is to help patients identify and change these core beliefs through weekly sessions with a therapist. In these sessions, patients are taught to identify negative thoughts and reactions, test those thoughts for accuracy, and replace those thoughts with positive ones. The core belief in cognitive therapy is that negative thoughts illicit maladaptive emotions.

SCHEMA THERAPY

Jeffrey Young, PhD, originally worked closely with Dr. Beck, the pioneer of cognitive therapy. While working with patients, Dr. Young found some had difficulty with the standard cognitive therapy approach. His attention turned to developing a therapy for those patients. In schema therapy, he combined existing approaches, including cognitive therapy and psychoanalytic therapies, into a three-stage approach: assessment phase, emotional awareness and experiential phase, and the behavioral change phase.

MEDICAL INTERVENTIONS

There is no medication approved for use for BPD by the US Food and Drug Administration. However, antipsychotic medications such as Haldol, Abilify, Risperdal, and Seroquel are often used to treat coexisting conditions such as depression and anxiety. Mood stabilizers are often tried when a patient has co-occurring bipolar disorder. The use of omega-3 fatty acids to reduce depression and aggression in women with BPD is currently being studied.

Living with BPD

When you consider there are 256 ways to meet the criteria for BPD, and only four different labeled types of presenting BPD personalities, you can assume that BPD looks very different in each patient. It makes sense then that while there are currently quite a few popular treatments for BPD, not everyone will have the same experience or the same results. Patients need to be self-aware of their progress and whether a certain approach is working. They need to feel safe with their therapist(s), and able to voice when a certain therapy approach isn't working. Likewise, it is imperative for a therapist to speak up when they see treatment not working or their patient experiencing an increase in symptomatology. These instances shouldn't be seen as failure. They are simply an opportunity to find a different approach that will better suit individual needs.

This difficult balance can be especially hard to find when a patient has co-occurring disorders. Sometimes it is hard to know where to start. Sometimes medication issues will get in the way. Sometimes one particular symptom will be particularly unbearable or even dangerous at a given time. It's important for the patient, the family, and the therapist to all work together and to take it each week, or even each day, at a time. Communication, support, and validation are the keys to being successful, no matter what treatment approach is taken.

PART 2

PERSONAL STORIES

What follows are stories from the front lines of BPD, penned by individuals who have been directly affected by this frustrating and sometimes mysterious condition. There is a lot of heartbreak here, but also success and triumph—whether it's the relief a diagnosis can bring or finding the joy in the often difficult recovery process. Within these essays, people with BPD have struggled to find the help they need—to connect with professionals they could trust. They have fallen to rock bottom, whether suddenly or slowly, and they have journeyed back to the surface. Some reveal how early signs of BPD were apparent in adolescence, while a few buried childhood trauma and avoided the full-blown effects of BPD until adulthood. Consider this a safe space—in which other people with BPD, their loved ones, and those who treat them explore the highs and lows of BPD, and share how they ultimately gained sources of support, help, and guidance.

I Am Not My Disorder

By T. J.

My name is T. J. I'm currently 38 years old and I was diagnosed with borderline personality disorder just last year. Throughout this journey of self-discovery and mental health recovery, I have been to see countless therapists. There was the one who didn't speak or ask me questions for entire sessions, then Debra, Maria, Vicky, Roseanne (all lovely, but things didn't work out with them), couple's counseling three times, and several individual sessions in between. I didn't know how to be honest and open, so I never got really far with many of them, and couple's counseling was seemingly pointless when I didn't even understand myself.

I don't recall experiencing symptoms in my early childhood—and I'm not sure when the onset of disorders truly took place—but my teenage years were more than rebellious; they were downright troublesome. I didn't run away to hang out with friends and have fun; there was nothing fun about running away, the world was so big and frightening. I ran away to put distance between myself and a world in which I didn't fit, a world where I was deemed a horrible person. I ran away to try to find something that would fill the voids inside of me and silence the chatter in my head—chatter that told me I wasn't good enough and made dying seem enticing.

Though diagnosed later in life, T. J. can recall moments from adolescence that were seemingly telltale signs of BPD. If you've been diagnosed, are there any moments you can remember from childhood that resonate with your diagnosis?

In life, I often felt like a puppet, rudely pushed around and manipulated to live the way my masters wanted or needed me to. While a part of me wasn't happy with this, I simply didn't know how else to live on a daily basis. The proverbial "good life" wasn't for me. I went through the motions: graduating high school, getting married at 18, having two children before buying our first house at 20 years old, having another child, and then attempting to get sober at 26, in the middle of a nasty divorce. With all of the preceding eight years of adulthood feeling like a nightmare, my saving graces were my children and my dogs. All of those milestones, and yet I still hadn't found myself.

I'm now able to recognize the walls, smells, paintings, fixtures, furniture, and food at a handful of clinics, hospitals, and rehab centers—after being admitted several times for drinking, depression, suicide gestures (which I had originally spoken of as "suicide attempts" and later admitted were cries for help), as well as nervous breakdowns. I was full of anxiety and fear. Nobody seemed to understand me. My world was dark, black, and suffocating.

The only place to go was up out of the hole, but the question was how. Who could help me? It was time for change—time to get open and honest in therapy.

My life was a tornado. I thrived in chaos. It didn't feel crazy, it just was. The world could see my storm clouds from miles away, but in the midst of my tumultuous twists and turns, I was obliviously calm. I did not know what I did not know. I was always striving for complete daily happiness and failing miserably. But that misery was an old friend. I had come to accept that this was my life—doomed, in darkness, and scattered with temporary joys.

I had enough friends and acquaintances to *appear* social and thriving. A coworker once commented, "I thought you were someone who had it all together. I couldn't be more wrong." Later, a once-very-special friend of mine (we stopped talking shortly after this exchange) offered a profound truth to me, "You have hurt every person who has ever loved you." I was dumbfounded. I wanted to argue back, but my mind quickly flashed to face after face, name after name of those who I thought had hurt me, but in reality, I had hurt. I knew she was right.

For me, "getting better" involved a culmination of efforts on my part, as well as outside support from family and friends. For starters, I finally became sober three years ago. I found my way to a 12-step program. I came to realize that alcohol could no longer do for me what I needed it to do—help me feel numb or feel better. With the newfound clarity that sobriety brings (ready or not), my failures glared wildly in my face: job losses, family fights, breakups, and burning bridges with important people in my life, among many other troubling instances.

In this early sobriety, I found myself vulnerable, stark naked to my core belief of not being good enough, with nowhere to run or hide. The only place to go was up out of the hole, but the question was how. Who could help me? It was time for change—time to get open and honest in therapy.

In three years, my diagnosis formed and evolved: depression, suicidal thoughts, self-esteem issues, impulsivity, codependency, fear of abandonment, addictive behaviors, sexual abuse survivor, and PTSD due to countless traumas I had tried so hard to dismiss, get over, or move on from on my own. I had trouble following through on tasks and healthy commitments. My frequently missed appointments, sometimes for no reason at all, became another red flag for my therapist.

"I'm adding borderline personality disorder to your diagnosis." She was ever so gentle about it. She reiterated my patterns: the black-and-white, all-or-nothing thinking; the impulsivity with which I made important decisions on my own; and my deal-with-consequences-later outlook. I listened and nodded in agreement and understanding. But I hadn't seen it coming. It began as a general mood disorder. I had blamed my disorder on my symptoms. I hadn't realized my mood disorder, or any disorder, was the *reason* for my symptoms.

Prior to this session, I had casually mentioned that I stopped taking the medication for my mood disorder and depression, and had been off the medications for several weeks. I was pretty confident that I was justified in doing so, but to my therapist, this was a problematic pattern. When I was originally prescribed medication for depression, I didn't like it; it made me too tired. Thankfully, my psychiatrist was patient with me. We went back and forth for several months. The medicine would make me too tired, so he'd decrease it. We'd switch the times of day that I took it, from bedtime to dinnertime to early afternoon. Soon, I had decided on my own that I'd take it around noon and then decrease it and change it according to my daily schedule with work and kids. In short, I hardly gave the medicine a chance to work.

I was impatient with the schedule. It didn't seem to be working, I thought. I hated having to take medicine at all, fearing that I'd have to take it for the rest of my life. I wanted to be in control, and I did not want to have to be tied to a medication schedule. It was the commitment I was having trouble with, not so much the side effects. I'd forget to take the medicine at all, or would decide that I'd take it later in the day but would then forget and it would be too late if I did remember it—the excuses went on and on, until even *I* could hear the patterns through their disguises.

Have you, or your loved one, experienced similar frustrations over medication?

My therapist understood my frustration. "Just let your psychiatrist know," she firmly suggested. When I broke the news, my psychiatrist was clearly disappointed and somewhat shocked that I had stopped the medication weeks earlier and hadn't informed him. I hadn't wanted to bother him with my inconsistent and frequent changes. In retrospect, I realize sharing those irregular changes with my prescribing doctor and therapist was important so they could properly diagnose me.

The "Look, a squirrel!" joke, commonly used to joke about ADHD, became increasingly familiar and less funny with every passing scatterbrained and distracted moment of my life. Some days, I'd wake up feeling brilliant and ready to take on the world, 16 tasks written out, completed, and checked off. By dinner, I'd be understandably tired. The next day, darkness would set in again and I'd wonder if my life would ever feel good again.

When my therapist suggested I try a newly formed eight-week intensive outpatient program for men that taught coping skills for trauma, anxiety, and depression, I was ready for anything that might help. Of course, I had my reservations and hesitations: Would I really be able to show up daily for a healthy commitment when I had trouble showing up to my individual therapy sessions? The last time I had been to group therapy was in a rehab setting and I didn't recall having learned much. I certainly hadn't opened up to the group.

It turns out I was more than willing to show up. While the daily routine was helpful, the support and understanding from the other men in the group, who had all been diagnosed with the same disorder or something similar, were a tremendous help. Every day, we processed as a group for three hours. I was no longer alone in my troubles. We learned how our brains work and why they work differently, as well as coping skills that we were encouraged to use in group sessions and out in the "real world." We practiced grounding and mindfulness techniques, used contracting to build better communication, and shared positive affirmations. I also learned that not only is it okay for men to cry, but it's healthy and healing. I watched in awe, throughout the eight weeks, as I became emotionally strong, more confident, more productive, and was beginning to make great progress with my close relationships.

One of the most important things I learned, and that I will take with me through life, is knowing that I am not my disorder.

Being diagnosed with BPD, and accepting it, has been so helpful in my recovery. I am not ashamed, but instead am grateful to have an understanding of how I work. One of the most important things I learned, and that I will take with me through life, is knowing that I am not my disorder.

My closest family and friends have a better understanding, and are able to help me in difficult moments by using simple reminders and key words like "grounding" or "mindfulness." We are now able to laugh through the hard times, instead of me acting out and making things worse. I am being kind to myself now. I know that the fun-loving person I am can live on, and the disorder I live with can now take a backseat.

T. J. is a visual artist and writer, married with four children, and resides in central New Jersey. Diagnosed with BPD last year, he has recently completed an intensive outpatient program focused on coping skills for living with the disorder.

Redefining BPD

By Edward Dantes

When I was 18, my mother and I sought professional help after years of emotional abuse at the hands of my father.

In our first session, the therapist said, "It sounds to me like your father has a personality disorder. You know, there are normal people, there are those who are a little bit outside our societal norms, and then there are people who are really beyond the pale. Within this last group are the ones we call 'personality disordered.' These people are very difficult to help, and many therapists consider them untreatable."

Being unfamiliar with "personality disorders," my mom and I didn't quite know what to make of this. But as much as my father had mistreated us, I still disliked this therapist's cavalier labeling of someone he had never even met.

Later, at age 20, I became suicidal and had to be involuntarily committed to a psychiatric hospital. During one group therapy session inside the hospital, the psychiatrist announced authoritatively,

"Mood disorders are 'biologically based' mental illnesses," surveying the 15 young adults in front of him. "But while these disorders might be biological, it doesn't mean you can't manage them effectively."

My mind reacted explosively. *How could you possibly know this? What evidence do you have?* I desperately wanted to shout at him. But I remained silent, slouching backward in my chair.

These snapshots encapsulate the hopeless viewpoint and fear of labels with which psychiatry inundated me. It would take everything I had to eventually break free from the resulting fear and despair.

How I Became "Borderline": A Very Brief History

As of this writing, I am 29 years old. I grew up in a family of four on the east coast of the United States. My father worked a demanding financial sector job, and my mother taught school part-time while caring for my younger sister and me. Our childhood was marked by isolation, emotional deprivation, and physical abuse. Starting when I was six, my father frequently beat me for small infractions, but was otherwise emotionally distant. My mother tried to protect me, but was too afraid and insecure to be of much help.

By my late teens, I felt depressed, scared, and helpless. Despite doing well in school, I had no close friends and didn't know how to talk to girls. The pressure to leave home and function as an adult felt incredibly threatening. At the same time, my father's mental health was deteriorating, leading him to be hospitalized multiple times for manic episodes and suicidal depression.

Some people with BPD might identify as "borderlines," but this is rare and a personal choice. Although the term borderline *is used throughout, this is not the preferred terminology, and care should be taken to avoid referring to individuals by their diagnosis.*

As our family life broke down, things felt increasingly hopeless. I felt furious at my parents, and suffered intense mood swings of rage, emptiness, depression, and terror. I wanted to get help, but couldn't trust anyone and kept everything buried inside.

Eventually, I became suicidal. After concocting a plan to kill myself—that almost succeeded—I was involuntarily hospitalized. This episode led to the diagnosis of BPD, given to me by a psychiatrist at the hospital.

Phase One: A Life Sentence?

In the year after my hospitalization, I extensively researched my "illness." Most readers will be familiar with the core borderline traits: they include black-and-white thinking ("splitting"), self-damaging behaviors, impulsivity, fear of abandonment, and unstable interpersonal relationships.

Through interactions with psychiatrists, Internet forums, and pop psychology books, I found out the following about BPD:

- BPD is a lifelong mental illness; it can be managed but not cured.
- Due to their reputation for being manipulative and demanding, most borderlines are avoided by therapists.

I became possessed by the fear of being a borderline, of having a lifelong mental illness that was difficult, if not impossible, to cure.

- Twin studies show that 50 percent or more of vulnerability for BPD is transmitted through the genes.
- Brain imaging reveals that the brains of borderlines differ significantly from the brains of neurotypicals.
- Borderlines suffer from a constitutional deficit that prevents them from regulating their emotions like normal people.

As a young person, I didn't know how to evaluate this data. If a person had PhD or MD by their name, or simply sounded authoritative, I tended to believe what they said. As I was already vulnerable, these ideas heightened my terror. I became possessed by the fear of being a borderline, of having a lifelong mental illness that was difficult, if not impossible, to cure. I was not only facing real difficulties, like my father's abuse and a lack of social skills, but was also impeded by the intense anxiety and negative expectations focused around the label "BPD."

A new BPD diagnosis can be confusing, but learning about the disorder itself is often overwhelming. Edward took a systematic, high-level approach to understanding BPD. What helps you make sense of BPD?

By the time I was 21, my parents had divorced and I'd chosen to live with my mother. For two years after my hospitalization, I was unable to work or attend college. Much of my time was spent at home, as I severely depressed, isolated, and brooding about being a hopeless borderline. But a sliver of hope survived. Part of me wanted to fight, to become alive, and to feel like a real person. When I had thoughts about BPD being hopeless, a voice inside my mind started saying, "They are lying to you!" I wasn't sure what this meant, but I wanted to find out.

Over time, I felt increasingly angry about the way borderlines were stigmatized. How could borderlines be so bad? Had none of them ever been "cured"? What if the things I'd read about borderlines were untrue, or the result of therapists who didn't know how to treat them?

Phase Two: "Borderlines Can Do Well"

With doubts surfacing, I began to research BPD in greater depth. Up to that point, I had received most of my information from psychiatrists and Internet forums—places where people spoke negatively about "their borderlines." I decided to go on Amazon and look for new information. The books that influenced me the most were, ironically, older psychoanalytic texts. The authors included James Masterson (*The Search for the Real Self*), Harold Searles (*My Work with Borderline Patients*), Gerald Adler (*Borderline Psychopathology and Its Treatment*), and Jeffrey Seinfeld (*The Bad Object*).

As I read about borderlines in long-term therapy, I was shocked to realize that many had fully recovered. Case studies showed people starting out hopeless and nonfunctional, but becoming able to work productively and enjoy relationships. It was clear from the narratives that these borderlines were coming to trust others, working through their pain, and coming alive. Given enough time and support, former borderlines could improve greatly and even be "cured." I remember thinking, "Wow, a lot of what I've been told about BPD is completely wrong; this is not a hopeless condition! If other borderlines can recover, why can't I do it?" I finally had some hope.

This burst of hope inspired me to seek help. I pursued psychodynamic therapy, interviewed several therapists, and found a kind psychologist who had worked with many trauma survivors. I went to see her twice a week for several years. Gradually, painstakingly, I made progress. Through reading accounts of borderlines recovering, and discussing the fears around diagnosis with my therapist, my anxiety and hopelessness lessened. Using online groups like Meetup, I tentatively started to seek out people my age to build relationships and venture out of my comfort zone.

I formed a strong bond with this therapist, coming to trust someone deeply for the first time. For the first time ever, I had periods of feeling calm. Being "re-parented" by my therapist, taking in her love, was one of the most important steps in my recovery.

Feeling more capable, I earned a professional qualification and began teaching sports to young children. The more time I spent around energetic kids, the harder it was to remain pessimistic. Being still a child at heart, I found a talent for relating to children on their level.

I remember thinking, "Wow, a lot of what I've been told about BPD is completely wrong; this is not a hopeless condition!"

Phase Three: "My Way of Thinking about BPD Doesn't Make Sense"

In difficult times, I continued to worry about the pessimists who said full recovery from BPD was impossible. The label still felt real. I was still thinking of things in terms of "borderlines are this, borderlines are that, borderlines can do well, borderlines can't do well, and so on." But with life experience, I began to doubt BPD. I wondered if BPD—the disorder, not the symptoms—really existed at all. The following questions became increasingly problematic:

- How can therapists reliably determine the degree of a given symptom that warrants its inclusion in a BPD diagnosis? For example, who can say when someone's relationships are unstable enough, or when a person feels empty enough, to cross the threshold and suddenly become a borderline symptom? The subjective nature of BPD symptoms seemed like a major weakness. For instance, Person A could have symptoms 1 through 5 from the *DSM-IV*, and Person B could have symptoms 5 through 9. The people might even be very different in how they express the symptom they share in common. Do persons A and B really have the same "disorder"?

- Did researchers have strong evidence that BPD was genetically transmitted, or that brain differences between borderline and "normal" were caused by biology?
- Why does BPD have 9 symptoms? Why not 4 or 23 or 87? How was BPD's existence as a 9-symptom "illness" first inferred?

As far as I was concerned, there were no satisfying answers to these questions.

Phase Four: "I Don't Need BPD Anymore"

Something felt fishy about the entire psychiatric labeling system. I suspected that BPD, along with the other labels, represented a house of cards that would collapse under close examination. More research was in order.

This time, I discovered a group of writers, including Stuart Kirk (*Making Us Crazy*), Paula Caplan (*They Say You're Crazy*), Jay Joseph (*The Gene Illusion*), John Read (*Models of Madness*), Barry Duncan (*The Heroic Client*), Mary Boyle (*Schizophrenia: A Scientific Delusion?*), and Richard Bentall (*Madness Explained*). From their writing and through observing myself, I came to a few conclusions.

While all the borderline symptoms are real in different degrees and varieties, I felt BPD itself is not a reliable or valid syndrome. In other words, I found no evidence that the symptoms labeled "BPD" occur together in people more frequently than would be expected based on chance alone. No one can reliably draw a line for any of the borderline symptoms beyond which one is "borderline" and before which one is "normal." In other words, the subjective, descriptive nature of borderline symptoms fatally undermines their reliability.

While my younger self had feared BPD as an incurable, genetically based "illness," by the time I was 25, my thinking had evolved radically. If the placeholder "BPD" was a nonexistent ghost, then many of the things I'd feared ceased to have meaning. It didn't make sense anymore to worry about getting better from BPD.

This is how I think about "borderline personality disorder" now: as a ghost, a fiction, a simulacrum, a figment of psychiatrists' imaginations. In asserting this, I am never saying people's painful experiences are not real. They absolutely are. But affirming people's pain is very different from arguing that BPD exists as a distinct "illness."

For Edward, labels don't help. But some experience immense relief in putting a "face" to BPD. What might be the pros and cons of each?

Further Emotional Growth

As I increasingly separated from the label "borderline," I continued to grow emotionally. Based on my work teaching children, I started my own business, which involved advertising, accounting, hiring staff, and communications. I moved into my own house, living independently for the first time, while continuing to socialize more. I was happy a lot of the time.

In my late 20s, I had my first real relationship with a woman. She was an attractive college girl; we had several interests in common and got along well. After the hopelessness stemming from my abuse and the BPD label, loving another person had seemed like an impossible dream. I was glad to be proven wrong. Loving her was better than I had ever imagined! This relationship was a first in many ways, teaching me a lot about emotional and physical intimacy.

I realized how, during the long years dominated by fear, despair, and anger, I had missed out on the best things in life. I realized more deeply that believing in "borderline personality disorder" had only held me back.

A New Way of Thinking

If BPD didn't exist, how could I understand my past borderline symptoms? The black-and-white thinking, emptiness, despair, fear, and rage had been very real. To understand them without the BPD label, I needed a new model of reality. I started by picturing distressing thoughts and feelings existing along a continuum of severity.

In my new thinking, each symptom was no longer "borderline" or "not borderline"; rather, my feelings and thoughts were the result of individual, unique difficulties in relating to and adapting to the world. In particular, I needed to understand how my father's physical abuse and my mother's lack of emotional availability had contributed to my problems. In this way, my past started to hold meaning, whereas calling myself "borderline" didn't really explain anything.

I modeled some of my thinking after Lawrence Hedges, a California-based psychologist who rejects *DSM* labels in favor of a system called "Listening Perspectives." In this model, a person uses different modes of relating at different points in time. Hedges describes these levels as "organizing (a term to replace psychotic)," "symbiotic (to replace borderline)," "self-other (for narcissistic)," and "independence (for neurotic-healthy)." These terms do not denote distinct "disorders." Rather, they describe fluid ways of relating that fade into one another along a continuum, evolving based on environmental input, and involving other people in the external world. They are not intended to be scientific. A person will operate in different parts of this continuum at different times and with different people. In this model, one would never have a borderline or psychotic "disorder"; the words *organizing* and *symbiotic* would have no meaning outside of a specific relational–experiential context.

This way of thinking is not proven science, but it works for me, and it's far better than believing in what I consider the static, hopeless "borderline personality disorder." Most of the time now, I don't even think about BPD. I'm more interested in real things.

Helping Others Break Free

Two years ago, I revisited some Internet forums about BPD that I had first seen as a teenager. To my surprise, these forums were alive and well; more people than ever were discussing such weighty topics as:

- What's the best way to manage your borderline?
- How do you fill your spare time when you have BPD?
- Can I have borderline, schizoid, and antisocial personality disorders at once?
- Why won't my family take my BPD seriously?
- Do borderlines have a conscience?

- Are borderlines more sensitive than the average person?
- Are borderlines more sexual than the average person?
- If BPD is biologically based, why do people blame us?
- You know you're a borderline when . . .

After seeing these forums, I started a website telling my story of hope and critiquing the medical model of BPD. This project has allowed me to learn from many other people so diagnosed; it has reinforced my conviction that people labeled "borderline" don't have the same "illness." Rather, they are unique individuals, most of whom have had very difficult lives. All of them want to understand their problems and get better. They are essentially good people with good hearts.

My message to them is that you don't have to understand yourself through the label of "BPD." In my experience, full recovery and healing from so-called borderline symptoms is absolutely possible.

For some reason, people tend to like these ideas a lot better than the prospect of managing a lifelong "personality disorder."

Edward Dantes is a young professional living near Washington, DC. He was diagnosed about 10 years ago and suffered from all nine symptoms of BPD. He is currently functioning and feeling well, and no longer meets criteria for the diagnosis. Edward now works to encourage other people struggling with BPD that full recovery is possible.

Editor's note: Oftentimes, fear of psychiatric labels will cause someone to avoid seeking help. In Edward's case, this fear, and the negative stigma surrounding BPD, led him down paths that almost cost him his life. Some of his statements reflect older models of defining BPD, such as the thought that it can be managed but not cured. It is widely becoming accepted that with proper treatments and patient participation and support, many can overcome pathological symptomatology. Edward chose to focus not on the "BPD" label, but on the problematic symptoms he had. In the end, the treatment he sought out and stuck with worked for him to better his quality of life. It should be noted: while there is more work to do in terms of defining BPD, the prior criteria for personality disorders given in the *DSM-IV-TR* is still the strongest empirically supported and valid diagnostic criteria.

This piece was adapted from "How I Triumphed over Borderline Personality Disorder," originally published March 26, 2015, at bpdtransformation .wordpress.com.

You'll Never Understand

By Brittany

"You'll just never understand." That is a line I have used and continue to use frequently. Because the truth is, who could understand? Certainly not a friend or a spouse, and definitely not a parent or a sibling. I live in a confusing, frightening, and yet beautiful world: a roller coaster of black and white with no in-between; a deeply intricate distribution of chaos. But most importantly, it is the profoundly difficult upheaval that I carry in my day-to-day life. This is my life, and this is what it's like because I have borderline personality disorder.

According to the National Institute of Mental Health, borderline personality disorder is classified as: "A serious mental illness marked by unstable moods, behavior, and relationships." Yes, I agree, that is some of the issue. But it is so much more than the mediocre definition you find on the first page of thousands of search results. You see, any person can read a book or a web page that claims to know about all the inner workings of BPD. Any person can think they've got it down pat after three or four pages of a scholarly article. But the

I live in a confusing, frightening, and yet beautiful world.

truth is, nobody has any idea what a person with BPD experiences in a single day, or in a lifetime, unless they themselves have BPD. BPD can be defined in myriad ways, but it's not until you ride the roller coaster yourself that you begin to understand the complexity and pandemonium of BPD.

On an average day, one moment I'm riding the high of living an exhilarating life, the next moment I'm falling down the perilous hill of agony. In one day, I can experience such a switch in emotion a multitude of times.

And it doesn't end there. The real battle is in trying to suppress those feelings to avoid conflict—that is, if I can even recognize them. This is exceptionally hard, especially because my days—my minutes, even—are unpredictable. At any given point, one thing or another in my environment can become extremely triggering, overwhelming me with intense feelings of abandonment, or maybe rigid anger I feel justified in expressing. Or it might trigger the loneliness, the emptiness that encompasses my soul. Anything at any point in time has the potential to trigger the onset of those horrid feelings. And that is the frightening aspect of having BPD. Because, the truth is, I never really know what's next.

One significantly upsetting consequence of having BPD is the destruction that comes when I get too close to people that I love. My whole life, I had remained at a safe distance, never letting anyone into my life too far. No one really knew the real Brittany, probably because *I* never really knew the real Brittany. I felt that this was the proper way to live, but I was never actually experiencing true relationships.

However, that changed when I turned 18. I grew close to people who I hold in my heart to this day. I let down my guard and, for the first time in my life, allowed myself to be vulnerable. At first, it seemed like the greatest blessing in my life to have such close relationships with people I felt so connected to. Unfortunately, as my good old friend Robert Frost once said, "Nothing gold can stay."

Making and keeping strong interpersonal connections can be difficult for people with BPD and for those around them. How has BPD interfered with relationships—platonic or romantic— for you or your loved one?

These people, who I placed on the highest pedestal I had ever known, began to pull away. They needed space from my overwhelming need for attention. Now that I look back with a more rational lens, I understand the need for space. However, back then, it stung more than words could describe. This pattern of them pulling away and me holding on tighter lasted for about a year, until many told me they couldn't do it anymore: My emotions got the best of our relationships. I was angry when space was needed—exceptionally hurt when time was given to others instead of me. I felt that I would be abandoned every single day. I felt an emptiness in my core when no one was available. People had consumed me, and I felt that I needed them in more ways than they could provide. After about a year, the turbulent relationships came to a screeching halt. And all at once, my deepest fear in this world, my fear of abandonment, became true.

Life went on after that. Some still kept in touch. I worked at maintaining some semblance of relationships, but nothing was ever the same. My days of feeling as high as the sky when friends were there

The depth with which I love can be so incredible.

and hitting rock bottom when they weren't were over. A sense of nothingness replaced the space in my heart where chaos had once resided. And that was that. I moved on with a bit of resentment and a quest for appreciation, but life didn't give me the eyes to be able to see with gratitude. And that, I feel, was the saddest aspect of the whole matter.

Today I've learned to work at maintaining some semblance of a decent life. I now go to dialectical behavior therapy (DBT), and work on using better tools to express myself. I work on trying to control my emotions and live life in a more effective way. I still hold my special friends close to my heart and hope that one day we could all have healthier, friendlier relationships. But that will only work if I do. For now, I avoid close relationships, because I don't yet have the capacity to maintain them. But my hopes are that one day, when I feel just a bit better and have a whole host of coping skills and dialectics under my belt, I will pursue more meaningful relationships. For now, though, I put them off limits.

The life of someone with BPD is beautifully disastrous. Well, at least my life is. While there are so many struggles of living with BPD, there are also a few positive aspects. For one thing, I feel things very deeply. The depth with which I love can be so incredible. I love both widely and deeply, and I don't know if many others could truly say the same. Because I feel so intensely, the happiness I experience is great because I can compare it to the pain I've experienced, which is also great. I have incredible insight into the inner workings of my being. When I am in a rational frame of mind, I can identify what I'm feeling, why I'm feeling it, and how my reactions both positively and negatively affect myself and those around me. And, last, my compassion for others is genuine. When I say, "I know how you feel," I literally know how someone feels, because I feel every emotion under the sun on a constant basis. I can be empathetic in the most authentic form.

Brittany describes some of the silver linings that can come with BPD. Can you identify any for yourself?

Although I struggle daily, I survive my difficulties with true strength. I still work to get through every day, from the moment I wake up to the moment I fall back asleep. Every day I do the best that I can, and that is the best I can do. But hey, isn't that all any of us can do?

Brittany is 19 years old and was diagnosed with BPD at 18. While life hadn't been easy for her before, the aftermath of a diagnosis brought on doubt. However, through support and DBT, she is learning to be a better version of herself every day.

Life after Loss

By Andy

My name is Andy, and I have bipolar II disorder as well as borderline personality disorder. This is my story.

I was originally diagnosed with major depressive disorder in college. After nearly flunking out of college, I graduated and went to law school. During that time, I started to notice that my emotions were out of control. I would take the slightest word as a major affront. The thought of scarring my body was extremely appealing. I engaged in binge drinking and reckless driving. I lied to my teachers, my friends, and my family.

Let's fast-forward to my marriage and my law practice. I hid finances from my wife and lied to her about them. Her slightest comment was a major attack to me. I was constantly angry and frayed. I was actively cutting and lying about how the cuts happened. At work, I was lying to clients and the court. I would recklessly push the envelope of how much I could delay things while I did not work, even on things I could have easily handled. I did not know what was

I didn't know that BPD was an actual diagnosis, I thought I
was being judged and found wanting.

going on with me, nor did I care. All this time, I was seeing my psychiatrist and taking pills for major depression.

Things got to the point where there were enough complaints that I was sent before the disciplinary commission. As part of those proceedings, the court-appointed psychologist diagnosed me as having borderline personality disorder. I didn't know that BPD was an actual diagnosis. I thought I was being judged and found wanting. I never mentioned this evaluation to anyone.

The lies got to the point where I could not keep them going. The fear of failing had me suicidal. My therapist stayed on the phone with me for over an hour while I took the train home and drove to the hospital. I called my wife to let her know I was in the hospital psych ward. Her response: "Thanks for ruining my life." I didn't speak with her for the rest of my hospitalization, nor did she come visit.

It's not uncommon to reject an initial BPD diagnosis, which led, in Andy's case, to a downward spiral. If you have BPD, have you had a similar experience? What eventually led you to seek treatment?

After all of this, I lost my wife and my law license, and still didn't know what was going on with me. I was in the hospital twelve times in five years. During that time, my diagnosis was changed to bipolar II disorder. I went through many different combinations of medications and two different courses of electroconvulsive therapy, which helped but did not keep things under control.

I went to what I consider "talk therapy" and was treated for depression. After a year with my therapist, he pushed me to try the therapy group he ran. He said he thought the group would help with my cognitive distortions. It turns out that the timing of my entry into the group coincided with several people leaving. I tried therapy group; it set me off every time I went.

After each session, the group went out to a restaurant to help us bond. I had difficulty attending group and would miss about a quarter of the sessions. After a couple of missed sessions, the group spent time talking about some of my issues. At the time, the major part of my "work" was trying to attend group. I didn't realize that, and the rest of the group members did not know that either. When we were discussing my issues, a couple group members started questioning the fact that I had difficulty attending, and asked why we were always dealing with my issues. I took it as a personal attack and not as the other group members working out their issues. I walked out of the group and away from that therapist at the same time. It was not until years later that I started to think he pushed me into the group because he needed members, not because it was the best therapy for me.

During this therapy, I went through a series of failed jobs. I worked at two different agencies selling insurance and doing financial planning. The problem was that I was afraid to talk to clients and push them for appointments. I quit my first position because I did not believe in the product or the methods of cold-calling people for Medicare supplements. I moved to a larger agency with a more recognized product. I still had problems contacting people and trying to convince them to have me out for an appointment and consultation. I lost that job after six months without sufficient productivity.

It was through DBT that I finally learned about myself—
and how to use skills to keep myself under control.

At that point, I decided to try car sales. I still did not realize that my mental health was keeping me from properly interacting with customers. I went through two dealerships where I was barely making a living. I started at a third dealership with a popular car brand with reasonably priced cars. I figured I would be able to sell these cars easily. I had problems at this dealership as well. I couldn't handle the stress. While the criticisms of my work was constructive, I took them as attacks. It was during this job that I was cutting and hospitalized five times in two years.

Each time I was hospitalized, I also went through a partial-hospitalization program that taught cognitive behavioral therapy, and an intensive outpatient program that taught DBT. After five attempts, the therapy still did not make sense to me; I couldn't make things work for me.

I was out of work as well as being in and out of hospitals. I had to apply for food stamps. The person handling my case started asking me questions and said it sounded like I was disabled and that I should file for Social Security Disability Insurance. I applied and it was determined that I was disabled due to borderline personality disorder. This time I spoke with my doctor about the diagnosis. He adjusted my medication and again sent me to a DBT course.

It was through DBT that I finally learned about myself—and how to use skills to keep myself under control. During the sixth course of DBT, I finally found a DBT therapist and have been going to him for over two years. At first, the goal was to keep me from cutting myself and out of the hospital. I am glad to say that now our goal is to work on quality-of-life issues, no longer issues of safety. My interpersonal skills are also improving.

I see my therapist weekly. He has told me that I have certain areas of DBT mastered, mostly observing, describing, and being nonjudgmental. I have developed better interpersonal skills, especially when it comes to my ex-wife. It took me a while to realize that my marriage was really a toxic relationship. However, because we have a daughter, I am forced to maintain a relationship with my ex-wife. DBT has helped me learn how to be more effective in my dealings with my ex, and how to explain my needs and wants in a productive manner. I've also learned to tolerate many of the comments that would normally push my buttons, accept that she is who she is and won't change, and that I will never be able to change her.

My story seems to be a success, but my journey is far from over.

Andy is 48 years old and divorced with a teenage daughter. His daughter is the most important person in his life. He was diagnosed with major depression in college. Distancing himself from people has been the ongoing story in his life. He graduated college and law school, and practiced law for 14 years. He lost his law practice and marriage due to his struggles while he was undiagnosed and untreated for BPD. He is now on disability and is being treated for compounding mental illnesses.

When Your Adolescent
Is Diagnosed

By Tabetha Martin

I was given custody of my sister in a whirlwind. Over a year after a major custody battle began between her parents, my sister began showing signs of the toll it had taken on her. I remember going to pick her up the day she was ordered into my custody. I hadn't seen her regularly for over a year—a stark contrast to being one of her primary caregivers until she was about eight years old.

I'd essentially been parenting since I was 12 years old. I cared for my sister after she was born, and then my brother as well when he was born two years later. I adopted my medically fragile son from the facility where I worked when he was four months old. Three years later, I gave birth to my daughter, so I also now had a biological child. I was currently a full-time student, a double major in nursing and psychology, with two young children. You name the child-rearing experience, I felt I'd had it. The custody battle between her parents had begun nearly two years earlier and now, suddenly, I was the guardian of an adolescent coming out of a hospital stay due to suicidal ideation. Nothing could prepare me for what was to come.

My sister walked into the lobby of the adolescent mental health wing to find her lawyer, our mother, and me standing there. She wanted nothing to do with our mother, and she did not trust her lawyer. You could see the internal push-pull she was experiencing in that moment looking at me. I'd always been the one she could rely on. Sure, I'd always been strict, but I was always there for her and loved her and doted on her. But I was standing there with two women she nearly despised. And suddenly she was being told she was coming to live with me. Later she told me she envisioned herself sleeping on my couch.

She and I left the hospital alone. I tried to joyfully welcome her without being overwhelming. I took her to the store to get her basic supplies and told her all about how we'd rushed to clear out a room for her. "What room? *My* room? Which room?" I told her that my daughter and son now shared a room, so she would have a room to herself. I saw her relief. Can you imagine? She was nearly a teenager and had her own room at each parent's house all her life. In reality, she was being spoiled as one parent tried to outdo the other. Each room was decorated. One even included her own bathroom. And now, suddenly, after the court battle and her hospitalization, neither parent's house was a place she could go back to.

I was prepared to raise a preteen. I was prepared to raise my sister. But something had happened in that year I'd barely seen her. Something was different. I didn't recognize this girl. She was beautiful, blonde with dark eyes, tall and elegant—those were all characteristics of the girl I knew and loved. But somehow her outgoing personality was muted. She would be fine and laughing one minute, and then turn her head away to hide the tears rolling down her face. She would be angry and lash out at seemingly simple issues. But then she'd act bubbly and loving afterward. She wasn't trustworthy and would take any length of lenience and run with it. Trying to parent her, teach her, was like hitting your head against a brick wall.

Parenting a teen can be difficult, even in best-case scenarios. If you're a parent, can you identify behavior that in hindsight led to your child's BPD diagnosis?

A court psychologist had been added to the case even before I was given custody. The psychologist did an in-depth family study. Each person in the immediate family had been evaluated, through a battery of tests and evaluations. About a month after my sister was placed with us, I called this psychologist.

After an argument in which my sister lashed out at my husband and called him names, I reacted and smacked her. I didn't know what to do. I was honest and straightforward with the psychologist: I was devastated. That's when she nonchalantly said, "Well, this is typical Borderline Personality behavior." I asked her to repeat what she'd said. I asked who had diagnosed my sister. I started to vaguely remember my mother mentioning the disorder. The psychologist told me that all three medical professionals who had seen my sister, along with the professionals she'd seen in the hospital, had all agreed. I hung up stunned. A BPD diagnosis for a child? I knew the term. I buried myself deep in studying anything I could get my hands on, reading day and night.

Suddenly, all the concerns I'd had when she was younger came flooding back. She'd been a deeply sensitive child, often upset at the smallest things, constantly fighting with her brother, and sometimes behaving inappropriately. While something had always nagged at me, any concerns I had expressed were promptly dismissed by our mother.

I realized I'd been parenting her all wrong. I was focused on fixing the problem behaviors, instead of reinforcing the good behaviors. Instead of yelling back at her in her fits of rage, I should have been leaving her to work them out herself. I should have made a point to validate her feelings, and listen intently to her, reflecting back what she said to me and using reflective listening. I should have been matching my tone and facial expressions with hers, in an attempt to show her I was connecting with her. Instead of raising my voice or forcing her to talk, I should have given us time to calm down. Instead of focusing on getting her integrated into school, I should have been focused on finding her the right therapist and treatment.

To be honest, we didn't find the right therapist. The therapist she began seeing was more of a friend, and ignored many ethical guidelines. We had no crisis plan. Any therapist seeing a patient with BPD should enlist the family and patient in making a crisis plan in case the time comes that it is needed, because that time always comes. It wasn't until after therapy started that my sister began cutting herself. In fact, the therapist discovered this and didn't mention it to me or work to enact a crisis plan. That is a clear sign the therapist isn't prepared. However, in changing therapists, you also risk triggering the fears of abandonment my sister so clearly displayed. It was a tough call on whether to keep this therapist or find a new one.

I'll tell you, this girl was determined and stubborn. Medications, knives, sharp objects, even chemicals were locked away. She still

I learned that people with BPD process things differently. They see everything as a threat, and their own bodies actually go into fight-or-flight mode.

managed to find things to harm herself with. I had her hospitalized right away when I discovered the behavior. It wasn't until we changed how we approached her and interacted with her that we saw a difference. I learned that people with BPD process things differently. They see everything as a threat, and their own bodies actually go into fight-or-flight mode. A simple comment can be perceived as a threat or incite fear of abandonment. Their reaction is not planned, and it is not manipulation; it is impulsive and reckless. And they regret it afterward, which then results in a cycle of shame and guilt. It is heartbreaking. As I began to see and understand this, I began to try to educate the people around us. But you can't put your child or teenager in a bubble, and outside influences do occur. Parenting a child with BPD, I had to learn to deny first instincts, to reprogram myself, and to not personalize *anything*. It is a huge practice in denying yourself, and learning to watch everything you say and do.

It was all so exhausting. I began a process of desensitizing myself. In my room, alone, on good days, I would visualize the things she would say or do that were hurtful or upsetting. I had to teach my body not to react. I also had to make sure I listened intently to her, empathized with her, and validated her emotions while not supporting any distorted thinking. Even so, it was just as important to always be authentic and truthful. Let me tell you, a person with BPD can spot a fake or a fraud. It was important that I avoided acting defensively, because in being defensive, I was essentially telling her that her feelings were wrong. A perception can be wrong, but feelings are never wrong to have, whether they are appropriate or not. It was difficult for me to hear her only recall bad memories from her childhood, and only rarely the good. I didn't understand that people with BPD have a neurological issue with storing memories. The amygdala, a structure in the brain, stores mostly emotional memories, and usually these are the negative ones.

In changing how we approached her, and life in general, we began to see her blossom and grow. Things were looking up. She began taking dance. This was a struggle in itself, as she was very hard on herself. She was constantly comparing herself to others, and if she didn't get a move right the first time, she would be visibly upset. We added extra private sessions with the instructor, who was very understanding. We worked with her on realizing that no one was going to be perfect without a lot of practice. They worked on moves and confidence. We had to take the same approach when she decided to play an instrument in band.

She struggled in school. In classes, she was afraid to ask questions; she was afraid she'd be viewed as stupid and often felt like the class was laughing at her. She took any negative comments from a teacher, not as constructive criticism but as a personal attack. She struggled making friends, as she was always afraid they would talk or laugh at her behind her back. In stressful moments, she finally told me that she heard voices in her head, often laughing at her, telling her bad things about herself. She was only able to maintain a single close friendship at a time, and only when she was that person's primary friend.

Through her struggles, we tried to talk about them and work on her perspectives. Then, I began to notice that her therapist was communicating with me through her, rather than directly to me. Why would a therapist treating someone, much less a child, with BPD do such a thing, especially knowing that perspective is a huge issue? Things were obviously interpreted unclearly.

Finally, her therapist became involved in the custody case—the very reason the judge had fired my sister's prior therapist. The therapist was doing parent and child sessions, but was also scheduling visitation herself. After a few visitation issues and my clear disapproval of her involvement in the case, suddenly, my sister's therapist wouldn't see her anymore. Not because my sister had done anything wrong, but because of the surrounding situation. This is probably the worst thing a therapist can do to a patient with BPD. Not only does it effectively trigger their issues and fears of abandonment, but it effectively solidifies these fears and further weakens any future therapist's chance to build trust with that patient.

Finding the right therapist can be a major frustration when seeking help for BPD, as BPD patients are often stigmatized as being difficult to work with. Tabetha learned to ask health professionals the right questions and was not afraid to let a therapist know when the relationship wasn't working.

I wish I could say things got better. In the aftermath of not only being unable to see the one person she'd confided in for two years, my sister's father also wasn't showing up or planning visitation. Our younger brother was going through a major surgery and expressed his severe depression with her. Being very empathetic and overwhelmed, she went downhill, quickly. She was hospitalized multiple times with suicidal and homicidal ideation.

People with BPD feel things very deeply, more than many other individuals. Their actions are not from a desire to manipulate, but from a place of very deep feeling and self-preservation.

One day, she ran away with a boy she'd met in the hospital. This was a relationship I'd discouraged from the start, but our mother had gone behind my back to encourage it, even going as far as arranging dinner between her, my sister, the boy, and the boy's father on a night that she had visitation. This undermined everything we'd worked toward: safety, trust, and openness.

When my sister ran away with this boy, it resulted in a countywide search. It involved police and search teams. Never did I think I'd ever be the parent whose child was being described on speaker from a helicopter. Both children had been hospitalized for suicidal behavior; both had been reading *Romeo and Juliet*. My sister was on daily medication, and I was concerned about her suddenly not having them.

After 12 hours, we found them. Finding her involved me chasing her down the street and tackling her. The police, right behind me, had to handcuff her. She was yelling, screaming, and assaulting the police officers. She was kicking the window of the patrol car from inside. She was placed under an involuntary psychiatric hold and sent to the hospital.

The court psychologist was concerned about my family and my children. She felt that my sister was a lost cause and that it was our mother's responsibility now to handle her. I had worked hard to get her Mental Health Individualized Education Plan in order. It was just about to go into effect, and I had had high hopes that this day therapy/schooling would be of great assistance. But it was all for naught. The judge ruled she would go back to our mother. Her father died suddenly less than two months later, and my sister turned to substance abuse to help her cope and numb her feelings. Our mother sent her to a specialized residential facility in another country until she turned 18. I was devastated and scared for her. She'd gone from a loving and involved home, to losing her therapist and then her father and being sent away from all family in a span of six months! I wasn't sure how she would interpret all that was happening.

People with BPD feel things very deeply, more than many other individuals. Their actions are not from a desire to manipulate, but from a place of very deep feeling and self-preservation. What I can tell you is that my sister is alive and well today. She is learning to live and build relationships in a healthy manner. I truly believe that having the right diagnosis, and the professionals sharing her diagnosis with us, is what gave us a fighting chance. I would have never known what to do or how to effectively parent her, help her, and love her in any meaningful way. Her diagnosis was a blessing. It was a shock and it was devastating, but it was also a blessing. It is because of this diagnosis we are able to have a healthy relationship today. It has been an incredibly rough road, but it is worth it.

A Mother's Heartbreak

By Amy Bursley

I am the mother of a 15-year-old girl with borderline personality disorder. I cannot express everything I have been through in just this small amount of space, but I will do my best to tell our story. Amber was born two months after my father passed away. She was my miracle baby, because she got me through my father dying of cancer, and she and I were always close. She started tae kwon do at the age of three, earning her black belt at age eight. She was into dance and theater, as well as volleyball and band. She was a very active girl who played French horn as naturally as her older sister.

It seemed she had everything going for her, but deep down inside she was a disaster waiting to happen. Her father was awarded primary custody of her in the divorce. Over the next eight years following the divorce, she systematically went downhill. She started having issues in school and hanging out with the wrong kids. Her grades started slipping, and her attitude was getting worse. Her father's way of dealing with her was to put her on medication to control her behaviors,

I felt helpless in this fight to find out why my daughter was slipping.

a never-ending game of *"Let's try this medication instead,"* or *"Let's just increase her meds to see if that controls her better."* During this time, she was in and out of seeing me on a consistent basis. She would go a month or two without wanting to see me.

At the age of 11, she met someone who taught her how to cut as a way to "release" that pain, or as a way to get high. She also started experimenting with drugs and alcohol. At this time, she wasn't seeing me, so I had no idea. She hid her cutting until one day her father found the cuts. He became more heavily involved with psychiatrists, adding even more drugs to combat it. While she was diagnosed with bipolar disorder at first because of her mood swings, it wasn't until she started cutting that she was diagnosed as having borderline personality disorder. This made a world of difference, because we could start using DBT skills to handle her behaviors and to help her learn coping mechanisms.

Despite therapy, things went downhill. I felt helpless in this fight to find out why my daughter was slipping. I wasn't kept in the loop a lot of the time, including how much medication she was on and for how long she had been taking it. This never-ending loop of psychiatric debacles and mistakes would make her condition that much worse. At one point she was on six medications and behaving like a mood-swinging zombie. She kept cutting and hiding it. I didn't know what to do when she would finally come back to my house. I felt so alone in trying to know who my own daughter was. She had quit her beloved band because she couldn't deal with the pressure. She had turned into someone I didn't know anymore.

I started to do some health-related things for myself to get ready for weight-loss surgery. I went to a nutritionist recommended by my doctor's office. I told her about my depression and anxiety, and she recommended I get genetic testing done, specifically looking for the MTHFR (methylenetetrahydrofolate reductase) gene mutation. I had no idea what she was talking about, but I went with it. Good thing I did; I ended up testing positive. In other words, something in my genetics was causing my depression and anxiety. I was prescribed Deplin, an active folate, and vitamin B12, specifically, methyl B12. This combination would link the missing pathways in my brain to create a more natural path for neurotransmitters to work properly.

Just like with psychiatric medications, there was no real "science" to getting the right dosage; it's a matter of just taking it to see what amount you need. I soon started taking my Deplin and B12 combo, and was feeling a lot better. I was happy and the anxiety was calmed. But I also had to play with the dosage to get everything right.

BPD or other personality disorders and conditions often present in families, throughout generations. Is there a similar link in your family?

Because I felt better, I started to think that maybe my daughter had the same genetic mutation. I mentioned this to her father. I fought him for five months on this; he reasoned that her doctors didn't know what I was talking about. Finally, he had the psychiatrist do the testing. Not only did she have the MTHFR gene mutation, but she had COMT (catechol-O-methyltransferase, which can cause panic disorder) and a few others. I was elated! At least now I was on my way to knowing what was causing my daughter to struggle.

She was soon prescribed the Deplin and methyl B12 combination and was doing better, even though she was still heavily medicated on Zoloft, Lamictal, Seroquel, and Vayarin. She would soon go on to have mood episodes at her father's home that resulted in her becoming violent and the cops being called. After these episodes, her father no longer wanted her at his house, because he was concerned for the safety of his other child. So she came to live with me as soon as she got out of the mental health facility.

I soon moved into an apartment with her, and things went well for a while, while she was adjusting. I would take her to school and pick her up. Six months went by, and then all hell broke loose. She had started cutting again and hiding it. Her grades started slipping and her attitude was worse. She ended up calling the suicide hotline and everyone came out. Police, fire, EMS, and social workers were all there to make sure that she was okay and that I was able to deal with what was going on. It was frightening. She went back into the hospital.

Her father and I had been looking into a more long-term solution and found a faith-based school that would wean her off the meds. Things seemed promising, even if I wasn't going to be seeing her for a while. Even if she didn't want to have anything to do with me, I wanted her to get better. She's been in this school now for five months. She has lost 20 pounds and is slowly coming off her meds without any cutting incidents.

My daughter is learning animal therapy, in which she's able to take care of horses and other farm animals. She is also still involved with DBT skills therapy. Giving her space has been the hardest thing to do, but I feel that it was necessary for both of us. I felt as though I failed her. I was in my own individual counseling up until this last year, when I fell into my own depression from the events that took place. I was learning coping skills to handle the extra stress but somehow I seem to have fallen off that course.

I would highly encourage anyone suffering from depression or anxiety, or who has been diagnosed with any type of mental illness, to be genetically tested. Everyone has different medication or therapy needs, but at least it's a start. Not knowing is the worst feeling in the world. You soon ask yourself, "Why am I like this?" and "What can I do to help my child not succumb to the terror of mental illness?" If, as parents, we don't know, then it makes that fight even worse. I hope mine and my daughter's story is familiar and helps someone who is in the same position that we once were in have a better, more enjoyable life.

Amy Bursley was born and raised in Austin, Texas. She has three daughters, one of whom has been diagnosed with BPD. In her spare time, she goes to the movies or to see live music. Writing is her true passion, and she's looking to accomplish so much more.

Radical Acceptance

By Ashley Emery

I dedicate this to my husband, whom I love with all my heart. Thank you for never giving up on me.

During the darkest time in my life, I was quite certain I knew how my life would end. My struggle had become a daily battle, and I felt the demons of guilt grasping at my throat. Every word that seemed to leave my mouth was angry and hateful. Emotional trauma and pain drenched me from head to toe. "Hopeless" doesn't begin to describe the feelings I held deep within every fiber of my being. I had nothing left to give. I was broken.

In all my brokenness and pain, somehow, I had to pick up my pieces. I had to care for the little humans who needed me, all the while weeping deep within my soul, overcome with guilt because of the thoughts that raced through my head—thoughts that paralyzed me with fear. I was planning my own death daily.

I pushed the thoughts down until I couldn't take it anymore.

I pushed the thoughts down until I couldn't take it anymore. I isolated myself within my dark bedroom; I ceased to exist to anyone outside my four walls. Everyone would be better off without me; all I thought I did was hurt the people I loved the most. I was so afraid to be alone and abandoned that I pushed everyone away first. If I could push them away before they decided to leave, then it was my decision. Somehow that made it easier in my head.

I felt myself pushing my friends away first. I quit calling. I started pushing my parents away, disagreeing with things just to start arguments. I pushed my husband away; in my mind I didn't deserve him anyway. I pushed my kids away. They deserved unconditional love; I couldn't give anyone anything. I was dead inside.

At this moment in my life, I had a choice to make. Either I was going to fight to get better or I was going to let BPD define my life. Stubborn to the core (a trait I come by honestly), I became determined to be the mother, the wife, and the daughter that I was created to be.

What made you seek help—for yourself, or loved one? Was it, as Ashley describes, her commitment to family, or was it something else?

During the dark times of my life, I didn't understand my diagnosis. More important, I didn't understand myself. BPD can be extremely hard to grasp because of the debilitating struggles with identity or sense of self. This struggle stems from problems regulating thoughts and emotions. In my case, my brain never shuts off. I struggle with basic emotional regulation. For example, a friend of mine recently called to set up a time for our kids to play together and for us hang out. We set a date about a week away that would be convenient for both of us. We were all excited to get together. However, as the day came closer, my moods fluctuated. I played out this event in my head over and over. What would we talk about? What would she want to vent about? What would my position on these possible issues be? I struggle with decisions and core value views to the point where they change sometimes rapidly. As I work through my thoughts on an issue, my views change because I feel like I could possibly relate to both sides. I try to understand every thought and action on such a deep level that it becomes complicated. So as the day came closer, I had to fight the urge to call and make excuses as to why I couldn't make it.

I have to mentally prepare myself for social get-togethers and meetings. It can become exhausting, and because of the emotionally draining process of preparation, I often have to cancel plans because I break down. After I break down, I experience horrible feelings of guilt and become incredibly irritating to everyone around me. It's a vicious cycle of unstable mood regulation.

If I can prepare myself to attend social gatherings, then comes the aftermath of the event. After I have finally trudged through the trenches of emotion I have encountered during an event, the next two to three days I go on a roller-coaster ride of emotions as I look back on every word said and every action taken.

Once I refused to let BPD control my future, I embarked on the most eye-opening journey of my life: the journey to mental health wellness. I spent countless hours researching BPD. As I researched, I would get depressed, because I saw a similar message in each page

I read: This fight was next to impossible, and women who struggle with BPD should not become mothers. The BPD-affected mother would pass this on genetically to her children and they would face irreparable damage to their emotional makeup. Reading that made me feel sick.

I dug deeper—not into research, but into myself. I began to understand that all of the research couldn't give me answers. It could, however, guide me in finding the answers within myself. I realized I can control how I let this affect my life, and as I educate myself, I gain wisdom in managing my own life. I am here to tell you that I still have bad days, but each day I get stronger. I rarely face such dark times nowadays.

It's important for me to make this clear: *It didn't just magically get better.* I hoped that maybe I would just make the choice to no longer be defined by BPD, and all of a sudden wake up and be normal. That's all I ever wanted to be. I was so fed up with feeling every emotion flood my body at uncontrollable speeds. No matter what my hopes were, it didn't change the fact that I had a long road ahead of me. During my journey, I would explore what mattered to me above all else: I was afraid of failing my children. I was afraid of losing my husband. I started to pay attention to my emotions and voice my concerns. I stopped the guilt trip before it even started. I was broken and I was going to heal; but it was not going to be easy.

Late one night while reading various blogs and articles about people struggling with BPD, I stumbled upon *The Dialectical Behavior Therapy Skills Workbook: Practical DBT Exercises for Learning Mindfulness, Interpersonal Effectiveness, Emotion Regulation & Distress Tolerance*, written by Matthew McKay, Jeffrey C. Wood, and Jeffrey Brantley. This book gave me hope and made me feel in control of my own path for once in my life.

After starting to repair myself and recognizing my destructive behaviors, the guilt set in again. I had tried to be a good mother the prior eight years. I loved my kids so deeply it hurt physically to think about all the times I had crushed them with my words. My children would come to me searching for approval and love, but I was so lost that I would push them away. When I pushed them away, I saw the disappointment in their eyes. It was killing me. I tried so hard to notice my emotions and stop the anger before it spread. Every time I tried to smother the fires of anger that burned inside, they would flare up and spread like wildfire. As I thought about a plan to tackle BPD and the anger that seemed to lurk deep in the darkness, I realized I could fight this.

That is when "radical acceptance" changed my life. Radical acceptance means you stop fighting reality and accept life in its current state for what it is. Life is ever-changing. My mother always says, "This too shall pass." I have heard my mother use this statement in times of hardship my entire life. I never knew what it meant until I started using radical acceptance daily.

BPD affects everyone in different ways. For me, every relationship is incredibly difficult. I constantly over-analyze every situation. Because I over-analyze, my mood and feelings toward any given topic change rapidly. Things are very black and white in my mind. I love deeply and hate angrily. I beat myself up emotionally with guilt every time I make a mistake—and guilt is a big issue for me. When it comes to guilt and radical acceptance, I look back to advice I was given as a young mother. One time, I was upset that plans I made to have an amazing day with my son had not worked out quite as I envisioned. As I let the emotion of failure pour over me, defeat was deep in my heart. As I explained to my mother how horrible I was feeling, she said to me, "Honey, there are very few Norman Rockwell

I fight because it's not over. It doesn't end here.

moments in life. You have to accept things the way they are." She was right; I dealt with the emotions of failure and soon was able to see that the day had not been wasted. In fact, some of my best memories today are when things *haven't* gone just as planned.

The way I use radical acceptance is through affirmations—to remind myself that whatever situation I am in, I have to accept it for what it is. Friendships are difficult because of my fear of abandonment. I have a hard time accepting irrational behavior or difficult situations. I trust too much and I get hurt. With this new acceptance, I have been able to protect myself from a lot of emotional pain.

During the messy trek down this long road of mental health wellness, I realized I needed to find my purpose. What was worth fighting for? Well, here it is: The best way to describe my house is organized chaos. My children are so full of life and energy—all six of them—and that is what I love about them. With all that life and energy also comes stress for me. Each day consists of an overwhelming roller coaster of emotions. Each one of them has their own little personality. I want to encourage them to grow. I want more than anything to support my children. My biggest fear today—and what drives me to never give up this fight—is missing out on all the blessings of happiness my children bring to my life. I sit and wonder when life is all said and done, what will I leave behind? What will my children remember about me?

I want them to remember a woman who never gave up. Who was strong in her faith, loved with all her heart, and even in times of struggle always persevered. I want to be the constant, the one they remember as always there to support them and help them.

All these deep, longing emotions that surround my desires to leave behind a legacy of love and purpose stem from the strong women who have impacted my life. My grandmothers have passed on lifelong lessons—lessons taught by example—in overcoming hardships, accepting circumstances, and ultimately persevering. I have taken many lessons of life to heart, and through my road to wellness I have leaned on them in times of need. Each of these influential women left me guidance to be the woman I am working to become. I knew that getting a grasp on my true purpose would save my life. Each time my cycle of destruction starts, when the thoughts start racing, I remind myself why I fight. I fight because it's not over. It doesn't end here.

Another issue I feel compelled to share is the need for a support system. Since learning about my disorder, I have done my best to educate the people around me. For instance, my husband always wanted to help me and he could see my struggle, but he didn't know how to help. After my husband better understood what I struggle with, we discussed ways he could help me. We came up with a plan; this way, when he now notices me struggling, he knows how he can help. In most cases, it's not that people aren't willing to help, it's that they don't know how to help. Now I work hard to communicate my needs to the ones I love. I work hard to educate them. Today, my support system is stronger than ever because they understand me.

I'm sharing my story to spread hope, and to knock down the walls and stigmas attached to mental illness. My message is that those of us who struggle with mental illness—whether it's BPD, anxiety, PTSD, or any of the other hundreds of labels used to describe these daily struggles we face—can heal. I was scared that my mental health would damage my ability to function as the woman I wanted to be. I am here to tell you that it doesn't have to. You are not alone in this; don't give up, because this fight is worth it. Find the joys in the things around you, even if it's a raindrop that lands upon your face.

If you are a parent of a person dealing with mental health problems, I would encourage you to educate yourself and get involved. Be supportive and don't give up. With education comes understanding, which is the first step to healing.

Ashley Emery is a 28-year-old mother who lives in southwest Washington with her husband Chris, five sons, and one daughter. Ashley grew up in the Pacific Northwest, moving often as a young child. She is an only child and remains close to both her parents.

Development and Diagnosis Later in Life

Mike Duperré

My name is Mike. I live in the Highlands of Scotland. Fourteen years ago, I was diagnosed with borderline personality disorder.

My illness began on May 25, 2001; I will remember that day for the rest of my life. I had met the woman of my dreams, my true soul mate. I had never had any girlfriends and never thought I ever would until Cheryl came along. On that day, the day of our engagement party, a relative who had abused me for many years during my childhood was invited—at that time, it was still a dark secret, never to be spoken of. He approached me in the bathroom that night and said something to me, bringing a wave of hellish memories and emotions to the surface.

When we went home that evening, I thought I was putting on a pretty good act of trying to pretend it didn't happen. But the next day, I was sick, crying uncontrollably, and didn't know what to do. What I didn't know then is that this was only the start of 14 years of the lowest lows, during which I would try to take my life because I couldn't live with myself anymore. Afterward, though, I would experience some considerable highs.

> *Like others, Mike has experienced strong physical and emotional reactions due to BPD. How would you describe your reactions?*

For me, BPD is pure torture. Every day, you're confronted by emotions you don't understand and are stronger than you have ever experienced. I experience dark thoughts about the way I perceive and believe others see me. Think of a dark hole whose walls are covered with hot tar; if you try to crawl out, you get covered in this hot, sticky mess. It's agony and you're going nowhere. You feel alone and that everyone hates you and that they all think that you are a disgusting person and would be better off dead.

I also have major anxiety problems; I am on medication to try to ease this and to help me sleep. Sometimes, the symptoms of BPD ease up a little, and I can cope with being alive and around people. The dark times come when the bad thoughts win. In the past, I have cut myself just to feel something—to relieve some of the intense emotions that course through me. I have also tried to take my life; something I now see was a mistake—something I hope I will never do again.

My treatment process has varied over the years. I tried one medication that made me feel like a zombie (that one was supposed to keep me from taking my own life) and another medication that made

When you're first diagnosed, it's not often you're told how the diagnosis will affect your life or those of the people you love.

---

everything worse. I have been on several drugs that eased some of the symptoms, but made me gain a lot of weight—an unfortunate side effect. Overall, a medication that eases some of the anxiety and makes me sleep works best for me. I have also had several psychiatrists and community mental health nurses involved in my care over the years, all of which used talk therapy. At times, this was helpful. At others, things got much worse.

Currently I am going through the STEPPS program (steppsforbpd .com). One of the first things we learn in the program is a new name for BPD: emotional intensity disorder. I feel this makes me sound less crazy and describes the condition better. STEPPS is based in a group setting; we started with 12 people and are now down to 4 (it's normal for people with BPD to struggle with the pressure of committing time and energy in a group environment). We meet as a group for two hours every week and individually with a mentor for an hour each week. My mentor gives me a lot of homework, which consists of workbooks relevant to the particular subject we learn about that week. For example, one worksheet involved digging into our negative thoughts and challenging them. In addition to homework, we fill out "continuum" sheets, which include two separate forms. On "pot forms," we record events that trigger extreme emotional responses. On the other form, we break down what our thoughts are and what challenges we can use to try and prevent an episode. I've realized that the more I put into the program, the more I'll get out of it. Through this form of therapy, I'm able to recognize what causes the flashes of emotions and break that down to prevent the intensity.

If you're in treatment, what works best for you? If you're seeking treatment, what are you hoping for?

Before I became ill, my life was good. I had a good job and a great girl, and most people liked me. But after 14 years with this illness, my relationships with family and friends have deteriorated. Unfortunately, looking at it from the outside, one of my episodes would look like I was rude and inconsiderate to be around (putting it mildly!). I would have outbursts of sheer rage and anger for no reason and could not communicate how I felt. I've had huge gaps in employment, and when I could get work, I found that BPD made things difficult, especially when working with others.

Relationships are especially hard for me—I constantly seek approval and reassurance from my peers, and when I don't get it, I automatically think I am doing a poor job and not performing. When I do receive praise, reassurance, and promotions, I never truly believe I am worth it and always think I'll screw it up.

When you're first diagnosed, it's not often you're told how the diagnosis will affect your life or those of the people you love. I regret every single bad thing I have done and remember them all; each one plays over and over in my mind, clear as the days they occurred. People with BPD will probably have experienced some form of this regret and shame. I am still to trying to make amends for the things that I have done during my illness, but it's frustrating when I can't make the people I hurt understand the impact a mental health

Don't be afraid; don't think this is the end, or that you are
alone. Don't think that nobody will understand how you are
feeling. Don't stop fighting.

disorder can have on an individual. It is *I* who did and said the
things, but it was the *me* in an emotional, irrational state that would
frustrate anyone.

But it's not all doom and gloom! I married my true love in front of
our loved ones; it was the best day of our lives and we will treasure
it forever. I often recall that day when I'm not feeling well and the
bad thoughts are creeping in. When I was first diagnosed, Cheryl
saw it as a positive thing—that we now knew what was wrong with
me. Still, getting a treatment that would help proved to be a very
long and painful experience. At the time of my diagnosis, I was in
a very dark place, and I think it's extremely difficult for loved ones
to see someone they love suffering so much and not know what to
say or do to help. Cheryl handled it as best she could, but struggled
with my illness. At times, I would be argumentative and would fly
off the handle at the slightest thing. I regret these events the most.
Eventually, Cheryl found a book called *Stop Walking on Eggshells* by
Paul T. Mason and Randi Kreger. It gave Cheryl and my parents
advice and ways to help. It turns out that the best way to deal with me
when I have an episode is to walk away and give me space until my
emotions calm down. It can be difficult for loved ones to just walk
away, especially when they are seeing their partners or loved ones in
a high emotional state and clearly suffering. It was for Cheryl, but

she eventually saw that by walking away, the episodes wouldn't last as long. It does help.

I love our two dogs and being part of the lives of our nieces and nephews—watching them grow up from wee babes into the adults they are becoming. My point is, this disorder is painful, but you are also able to deeply feel the joy and happiness in life, too. If you have just been diagnosed with BPD, I have this message for you: Don't be afraid; don't think this is the end, or that you are alone. Don't think that nobody will understand how you are feeling. Don't stop fighting.

It's natural to be afraid, especially of things out of your control—say, being trampled by a herd of elephants that escaped from a zoo, tsunamis, and earthquakes. But your diagnosis *is* in your control. It may not feel that way at times, but if you feed the beast, it will only get bigger. Try to distract yourself with thoughts that bring you peace, happiness, and joy, and that help you feel relaxed.

This is not the end, but rather the beginning of your recovery. No matter how long you have had symptoms, you now have a diagnosis. For some people, it takes years to receive a diagnosis. This is a positive thing; it means you will start to get the help you need to feel more like yourself and get well.

Know that you are not alone. There are many of us—and many who are more than happy to share our stories to show you just how *not alone* you are. Social media is an incredible tool and has shown me just how many people there are with BPD; their stories have given me the strength to write this for you now.

Also, never give up. If you give up, then you miss out on so many of the wonderful experiences life can bring, such as love, kids, and travel, to name a few.

I'm so glad you've taken the time to read this collection and hope you have the support system and services you need near you. Sometimes, you have to look really hard, but in the very least, you can receive counseling and support online, which is a great development for us with BPD.

Mike is 36 and lives in a small village in the Highlands of Scotland near the Moray Firth. He works as an IT specialist for a call center. In his spare time, he likes to play first-person shooter and role-playing games, as well as walk his dogs and go swimming.

It's Never Too Late to Recover

Betty B.

My life was in utter chaos for so long. I was terrified the day I walked into Northern Pines Mental Health Center. A cool breeze from outside followed me in. I took a big gulp of air and walked up to the counter. The receptionist kindly asked what sort of problem I needed help with. "I have anger issues, I'm married to an alcoholic, and I was molested," I told the receptionist. "I'm sick of living like this. I need help. Fix me." She handed me a pen and a clipboard with a packet of green and pink papers, and told me to have a seat in the waiting room.

I brushed back my long, black curls from my face and pulled my t-shirt down over my belly. As I scanned the room, looking for a vacant chair, through the window I saw an apartment building, some trees, a parking lot, and two dumpsters. I sat in the corner, on one of the dark green chairs lined up against the light beige wall.

The waiting room was full of people, and I thought for sure they were all judging me. The fluorescent lights glared down at me like an inquisitor's floodlight, exposing me. I glanced at the papers, and I felt like I was back in school. I hated school. When I was a kid, we moved so many times, and I could never do well on tests no matter how hard I studied. I took a gulp of air and started filling them out as best I could.

An hour later, a petite older woman in a dress came up the stairs to the waiting room and introduced herself to me. "Are you Betty? I'm Pat," she said. "My office is downstairs. Come this way." At the bottom of the stairs, a long white hallway dead-ended into an inter-section; we could go only left or right. She steered me to the second door on the right, to a small, cluttered office with a black love seat on one wall, a bookcase next to the window, two blue upholstered straight-back chairs on the other wall separated by a coffee table, and a desk with an office chair next to the door. From the window on the left side of the outside wall, there was a view of the parking lot. I sat on the chair closest to the desk and set my purse on the floor.

Pat asked me, "Can you tell me why you're here?"

I knew I had to talk about my past. I had been to a therapist 20 years before, but it became uncomfortable, so I quit. But as I grew older, I got sick of living with all the dysfunction and all the fighting. I was always fighting with my alcoholic husband, my kids, my friends, my mom and brother—you name it. I was angry with my brother and resentful because my family approved of him and criti-cized me. I had a big fight with my brother in the parking lot after my mother's funeral. Now when I see people arguing, it's embarrassing to me, because I was that person. I couldn't get along with anybody. I was always right; everybody else was wrong. I hated people. I couldn't talk to anyone without blowing up and being mean and sarcastic. Yet I felt sad when they hated me. What did I expect?

I was too old to fight! I lost my kids and grandkids, my friends—I lost everything! My teenage daughter didn't know where she fit in life. She was confused because I was too passive, and my friend of 30 years was too controlling. When I found out that my daughter was threatening suicide, I thought it was that controlling friend's fault. I busted into that friend's house, pushed her against the wall, and broke her computer. I slapped her. Because of this, I almost went to prison for 18 months.

"I need to deal with my past," I told Pat. ". . . I'm scared . . . I have four children from three different fathers. My family belittled me for that. My father was an alcoholic, and he died when I was nine years old. My mother had some kind of mental illness; I don't know what you call it. She was happy and mad and sad and angry. When I was in the seventh grade and my brother was in the eighth grade, Mom would take off for two weeks and leave us to fend for ourselves. We had to steal food. We moved around all the time."

I watched Pat to see how she would react. I thought for sure she would judge me, too. She looked serious and said, "That must have been hard."

It can be hard for people with BPD to trust a new therapist after having poor experiences with one in the past. Betty tried again and was able to find a therapist who actually helped her. If you've had an unfortunate experience with a therapist, how you were able to try to trust again? How could you help a loved one looking for a new therapist?

The other women in the group didn't make fun of me or call me names. In fact, we started joking and sharing with each other.

I agreed. I said, "I was so addicted to dysfunction. Guys cheated on me. The last one was abusive. I dated one nice guy, but he wasn't fun. I dropped him like a hot potato."

She asked me a bunch more questions, and said, "You meet all the criteria for borderline personality disorder. I think the best thing for you is DBT; that stands for dialectical behavior therapy. you will learn some skills to make you a stronger person, so that you can deal with the past. For now, we will only talk about your issues in the present."

I felt some relief, but I thought, "Why am I doing this DBT? I never heard of it before."

We met for about six weeks, and then the DBT skills group started. I was afraid of what the other members would think. I felt so dumb. It was like going back to school. But the other women in the group didn't make fun of me or call me names. In fact, we started joking and sharing with each other. I learned that I was not the only one who had to deal with not being listened to.

The first two weeks we talked about something called "mindfulness." I never heard of that before, either. It helped me to slow down my angry thoughts and to get myself out of "emotion mind" into "wise mind." "Emotion mind" is what I was in before DBT, all the time. I always saw things through the red cloud of my anger. "Reasonable mind" is what is needed when you are looking at facts, like how much money you have in the bank. (I wasn't good at that either.) And "wise mind" goes into my core to combine the emotion and the facts to come up with a decision that is right for me, that will make my life better in the long run.

During the next six months, I learned emotion regulation, distress tolerance, and interpersonal effectiveness skills. Every week I had assignments to do. Some weeks I was too tired from working a seven-day stretch. But if I didn't have my assignments done, I had to do them in session with Pat, who held me accountable. It was the kind of firm compassion I didn't get from my parents.

Those people skills really saved my life. Before DBT, my daughter had stopped talking to me and would not let me see her children because I was, as she said, "batshit crazy," and she didn't want her kids exposed to the yelling and swearing. While I was in DBT, my daughter started to talk to me again. She still didn't trust that I would stick with it. I never completed anything. And it was a yearlong program! I was still angry. I was pissed off at the world and everybody. I was mad at my coworker from the previous shift because she didn't start the residents' clothes washing. I complained about another woman in the DBT group because she fell asleep during group.

Pat told me, "Don't worry about what other people are doing. If you are trying harder than they are in therapy, you are the one who benefits. You are here to learn, not to change anyone else. Accept her the way she is." This was a new way of thinking for me. I started to see the connections between DBT and the Al-Anon program I was going to in order to cope with my husband. I recognized radical acceptance in the serenity prayer.

Like I said, I slowly learned over the course of that year in DBT to accept people as they are, to listen, and think before I speak, and to be nice to people instead of tearing them down. My daughter and I developed a relationship, and she let me visit my grandkids. The first day she let me babysit by myself, I was so happy; I had to call

I slowly learned over the course of that year in DBT to accept people as they are, to listen and think before I speak, and to be nice to people instead of tearing them down.

my therapist. I apologized to my daughter for being such a crazy mother. Lately she even thanked me for being a good person. I told my brother I forgave him, and spent his birthday with him.

While I went to Al-Anon, my husband attended Alcoholics Anonymous. He worked on his sobriety and on being a nicer person. We started doing projects together, and we started going to family gatherings together. We still get along. I'm a group representative in Al-Anon now.

The financial cost of DBT was hard for me. I was the sole wage earner for the family, and as a night-shift staff at a group home, I didn't make much. Insurance didn't cover it all, and I wound up in debt. Sometimes I got mad at Pat because she was making me work so hard. There were a couple times I wanted to walk out—especially after I finished DBT skills group, and I faced my past—being molested as a child and teen. But my goal was to get better, so I wasn't about to quit. I thought, "Where would that get me?" I wanted to prove people wrong. I thank DBT for giving me the life that I never had.

I'm enjoying my job now. By helping other people, I'm helping myself, too. The things that come out of my mouth are God-given—not the way I used to talk or think. I still use my skills and Al-Anon. I still call my sponsor. Sometimes I have doubts. I pray.

I was a weakling. I was so submissive. I was raised to feel like I was meant to be seen and not heard. When I told my mom stuff, like how I was molested, she didn't believe me. Now, I stand up for myself. I get shaky, and I don't like it, but I do it.

I still have bad days, but it's how I deal with them. I don't hold a grudge like I used to. Sometimes when people tell me something, it's not what I want to hear, but it's what I need to hear.

Betty B. is a mother of four children and grandmother of seven, living in Minnesota. Born in 1959, she grew up in the Midwest. She has been married to her current husband for 20 years and works as a peer specialist with people who have a mental illness.

BPD Awareness and Three Key Components of Recovery

By A. J. Mahari

Borderline personality disorder remains one of the most misunderstood challenges to the mental health of so many. In fact, the very traits used to define BPD are universally human traits, including feeling angry, fearing abandonment or loss, and experiencing shifts in mood, to name just a few. The difference in these and other traits adding up to a diagnosis of BPD is not the actual traits themselves. These traits define BPD when it is determined they are much more intensely felt and reacted to, as well as when they are frequently and more extremely experienced and manifested in problematic, abusive, and/or self-defeating expressions and/or behavior.

I was diagnosed with BPD at the age of 18, in 1975, by an angry psychiatrist in a very uncaring and punitive way. He did not explain

I was struggling with everything in my life, all my life.

BPD to me at all. As I was given this diagnosis, I was simultaneously told to leave his hospital because they could not help me. In 1975, there was no Internet. There was no awareness for people diagnosed with BPD or for loved ones of people like me.

I was struggling with everything in my life, all my life. When the psychiatrist labeled me BPD, with no explanation, I was triggered and experienced another abandonment, another betrayal, and dismissal. All my life, I had been dismissed when I needed help, support, and love from my family.

Have you felt similarly abandoned in your struggle with BPD? How do you cope?

I left home to begin college at the age of 17. I needed to get away from a mother and a father each with BPD and narcissistic personality disorder. I had not known nurturing, or affection, or emotional availability. I had been a very sensitive child in a family that had no idea what to do with emotions other than react with anger, devaluation, and all types of abuse.

When I arrived at college in Toronto, Canada, it took me all of two weeks before I realized I was lost and ill-prepared to cope with anything. I lived in a dorm across a bridge from a hospital. Within my first two weeks out in the world, I knew I had to walk across that bridge to the outpatient mental health clinic and find someone to talk to. I had no idea why. I was just so lost and overwhelmed, and

I was plagued by anxiety. I was angry and hurt, and didn't know it. I lacked so many skills and any knowledge of how to relate to others or myself in healthy or even remotely successful ways.

I spent the next decade talking to numerous social workers, psychologists, and psychiatrists, refusing all medication because I was too scared of pills to take them. Twelve years of my life—years in which my suffering was front and center inside of myself, and often aimed at others around me, almost on a daily basis—were lost and wasted. Despite this, I would continue to pursue athletics, at which I excelled, and courses in a wide variety of subjects. I had friends but really didn't know how to relate to them beyond surface stuff. I told untruths in attempts to hide my shame and my feelings of lostness and alienating differences, which left me void of any safety.

During that time, I stumbled through life, panic attack after panic attack, through depression, anger, and defensiveness. What I have long since known about this time in my life was that I saw the world and everyone in it (that I knew, lived with, went to school with) as an extension of the experience of my abusive and emotionally unavailable parents. I had no reference for my feelings. I was dissociated from all feelings except anger and hate. I grew up in a highly abusive and dysfunctional family. They had taught me nothing but how to fight—how to use conflict to try to meet needs.

I interacted with people as if I was a tough, know-it-all, intelligent (intellectually yes, emotionally—absolutely not!), competent, strong, and brave person. I didn't know who I was at all. I thought and believed that my high conflict and confrontation, along with intimidating style of trying to relate to others, meant I was strong. Looking back, I realize I was really a lost, scared, terrified person without a sense of self or identity. I did not know how to connect to people in ways that built relationships. I only knew what I had

Without a sense of self, there could not be any self-worth, self-respect, self-esteem, or self-care.

learned relationally from my parents: how to tear down what would have otherwise been attempts to connect.

Over those 12 years in and out of therapy (with no talk of, reference to, or recollection that I had been diagnosed with BPD), I was well aware that I was suffering and that something about everything in my life was not "right," was not okay, and was not working out. Yet, I felt absolutely powerless and helpless to change this. I kept talking to therapist after therapist, more to have my suffering witnessed and my never-ending rants of being wronged heard (without any awareness of how I was playing out the victimization) than anything else. I had suffered as a child because my parents, especially my mother, had no capacity to bond, nurture, validate, encourage, or help me know any kind of emotional safety. I lost my sense of self and lived without a container for that self. Instead I lived from and through an empty, angry, alienated, needy, punishing of self and others—a false self.

The lack of self left me acting out, raging, and manipulating others to rescue me emotionally and otherwise. I remained unsatisfied and ungrateful, unable to take in the kindness and help I, through my outlandish behavior, pulled for and at the same time rejected. I would later learn in therapy that I was wanting people to give me what my mother had not been able to; if I didn't get what I had lost and always wanted and needed from my mother, getting it from anyone else was not going to matter. It could not ever, at that point in my life, make up for all that was so empty, wounded, invalidated, and devalued.

Deep down, I wanted simultaneously to be seen and cared about, to be praised and liked, and to feel connected. But because all that was unsafe and not anything I could trust, I wanted to be left alone, to fight, and to tear apart people's efforts to care about or for me. I was my own worst enemy. I had become my own abuser and a very difficult (to nearly impossible) person for anyone to get close to or try to care for. Care equaled annihilation to me. This was the "get-away-no-come-closer," "I-hate-you-don't-leave-me" reality of being without any sense of "self." Without a sense of self, there could not be any self-worth, self-respect, self-esteem, or self-care. Without any of those crucial self qualities, I had no self or worth or anything remotely similar from which to relate to others.

Can you relate to the push and pull A. J. describes?

The human context of my experience growing up, experiencing emotionally arrested development and not knowing it, meant that I had only the ability to relate, act, and react emotionally to others from the perspective of a wounded and damaged young child, regardless of how old I got with each passing year. Getting older with the wounded quality that is BPD does not include emotionally maturing, at least not until one gets into helpful therapy.

In 1990, at the age of 32, I read *Toxic Parents* by Susan Forward. This marked the beginning of my journey and the process that would lead me to recovering from BPD in 1995 at the age of 37, just about to turn 38.

Toxic Parents led me to the beginning of understanding that my family was a toxic one. They had forever scapegoated me as being at fault for everything wrong in the family, but it wasn't my fault. This renewed in me a desire, equal to increased levels of fear and anxiety, to see another social worker. This social worker would not let me talk. All I had done in "therapy" was talk, talk, talk, and never listen. It is not, as I found out the hard way, at all possible to learn if one is not willing to listen to others who know more. This social worker would only direct me to draw pictures. I hated it! I couldn't draw. Shame engulfed me. I could talk; I was smart. I had an impressive, articulate way with words. What I didn't know then, though, was that all my endless talking was blocking me from gaining any awareness. I wasn't listening to anything anyone had to say.

I hated the drawing and not being allowed to talk, because talking was my (defensive) overall strength (or so I thought). I felt strong talking. I felt embarrassed and ashamed having to draw because I wasn't much good at it.

Then, a funny thing happened. An incredible forward-moving awareness began to emerge with this social worker, after years of no growth (which was my responsibility, not all those therapists; I was dancing as fast as I could and would not let them help me). I began to gain insight by drawing and listening to this social worker's questions about how I could then describe what I had drawn. She introduced me to themes and to listening to her thoughts. That began to free me slowly from my own talk, talk, talk. That was what was keeping me from much-needed awareness—the kind of awareness needed to be able to grow, the awareness of the process and the work of recovery.

This social worker asked to talk to my family doctor. Together, the two of them let me believe they were arranging for me to see a nutritionist. All I was truly aware of back then was that I was eating too much, and that, as a result, I had developed a painful ulcer and still couldn't stop eating. I ate to repress the pain and feelings I could not cope with and ended up weighing almost 400 pounds.

The social worker and the doctor basically tricked me into a five-day-per-week outpatient group therapy program. The reason I ended up being referred by the social worker and the doctor was because they knew better than I what I really needed. They had connected my compulsive overeating to my deeper emotional issues and to the BPD diagnosis following me around on paper from therapist to therapist (no one ever mentioned again to me that I had BPD until I would come back to it in group therapy). At the intake appointment, I thought I was talking to a nutritionist until I realized she was not mentioning my weight or food. She was asking me other questions. With my mounting confusion, I finally asked this woman, "What are you talking about?"

She answered me with her own look of confusion, when she said, "I've described our programs to you, and I am asking if you will agree to attend our outpatient, full-time, five-day-a-week, four-hours-a-day group therapy program."

I started to sweat. Anxiety overcame me. I was agoraphobic, painfully obese, lost, afraid, and hiding from the world (though I had a partner at the time). It was difficult for me to go out, to walk, both physically and emotionally, due to the cruel words of others.

And yet, when that question hung in the air for what seemed an eternity, I answered rather quickly. How could I possibly tolerate the anxiety that arose simply contemplating this, much less the anxiety if I agreed to it? How could I go to therapy and be around people every day for four hours? I had no idea how to cope with any of that. Yet, despite feeling betrayed and lied to by the social worker and doctor, I rather quickly replied, "Yes." Just one simple word: Yes. That was

Feel the fear, doubt it, devalue it, deny it, endure the anxiety . . . and say yes to therapy regardless.

the beginning of three rounds of the group therapy program over the next two-and-a-half years. It marked my willingness to move toward change, awareness, and so much more, but in that moment, all I felt was tremendous fear and anxiety.

The lesson here for others is this: Feel the fear, doubt it, devalue it, deny it, endure the anxiety, and so on, and say yes to therapy regardless. That's the way to journey toward getting better. The process of therapy that led to my recovery required exactly what I found: amazingly loving, dedicated, and skilled therapists. A key thing in my experience (that I now extend to my own clients, with some limits) is that they allowed me to be "borderline"—who I was—until I could learn more. Therapists must not expect people in incredible pain (whether they know they are in pain or not) and lacking in interpersonal skills to be able to behave better than they know how to. It was crucial in my recovery that, within some limits, I was given the space to act out, just as quickly learning that my acting out had consequences—consequences I had not ever realized or been taught, consequences that I would have to learn to own. What a motivating experiential way to learn, change, and grow.

I was blessed to have therapists in this eclectic modality group therapy I went through who continued to work with me—even through some of the most incredible resistance I presented to them in the process—without ever giving up on me. My recovery would also not have been possible without their boundary setting, no

Borderline personality is not an identity. It is not a
life sentence.

matter how much I initially fought it. Essentially, they provided me
with an external container that helped me access my inner child—an
inner child who, for the first time, experienced feeling safe. Through
a comprehensive program, for the first time in my life that lost and
dissociated-from inner child trusted—trusting them before I did.

The same year I began my recovery, I got online and built my
first couple of websites, borderlinepersonality.ca being one of them.
I decided to write about my experience and my recovery. I wanted to
help others. At that time, there were maybe two or three other small
sites on BPD, and one for loved ones of those with BPD.

I have been writing and working online for 20 years now. I now
counsel and coach clients with BPD, as well as family, loved ones,
and those who are the adult children of parents with BPD and/or
narcissistic personality disorder.

While many professionals, and many people, still do not believe
or fully acknowledge the possibility of recovering from BPD, it is also
the case that no one has completely explained, in any definitive way,
what recovery from BPD is, means, or looks like. Borderline personality is not an identity. It is not a life sentence. Recovery is possible.

All too many believe that DBT skills training is the only model of
recovery from BPD. It is not. It is helpful for many diagnosed with
BPD to learn skills to stop self-harm and find ways to not feel actively
suicidal. It is also much more, but a complete recovery model it is not.

A. J. shows us there doesn't have to be one single, fixed path toward recovery; not all methods will work for everyone, universally. DBT worked for Andy (see page 57) and others, but A. J.'s path was different.

Does anyone have *the* recovery model for BPD in any of the many treatment modalities for BPD? I don't think so. What I know, from my own recovery, is that what helps the most is being exposed to several different strategies and modalities of treatment in the recovery process. Which ones can be used for the most effective treatment really hinges on each individual with BPD.

Recovery from BPD, in my experience, has meant that I no longer meet the diagnostic criteria for BPD (see page 19). Some people have referred to no longer meeting the diagnostic requirements as their BPD having been "remitted," but I would define this as still being in an active process of recovery.

I would describe my full recovery from BPD, not just as no longer meeting the diagnostic traits I once met. What I mean by "recovered" is that I am today, and have been for 20 years now, a person with balanced IQ and EQ (emotional quotient). I am a person who is in the average mentally healthy place, where those who do not have (or have never had) a personality disorder live. I have a reasoned and not over-reactive style of relating, and my emotions are not triggered to dysregulation anymore. I have effectively become a person who has lived the last 20 years of my life as people who never had BPD do.

I know who I am. I found my lost, previously emotionally arrested inner child, my authentic self. I live in the here-and-now. I worked through the stockpile of anger, grief, and unmet needs of invalidation, lack of nurturing, and abuse that were the wounding aspects of how I developed BPD in the first place.

Three Key Elements of Recovery

In my opinion, full recovery from BPD is still not as common as it could be or should be, and it's unfortunate that there isn't much representation of actual full recovery from BPD on the Internet and in other sources. There is also a lack of research from professionals; they seem to lack the motivation to study and define BPD recovery. Since my own recovery from BPD and from my experience counseling those with BPD, I have learned to:

1. **Humanize each person with BPD** and see each individual in the context of their wounding human experience. Symptoms of BPD must be normalized as the defenses one needs to survive in early childhood—defenses that no longer are helpful in the here-and-now.

2. **Recognize the causation of BPD** is unmet needs, namely lack of nurture and an invalidating environment, resulting in an insecure, or lack of, bonding and attachment in early infancy and childhood. One must understand the connection between this perceived or actual experience—with or without abuse—and how it arrests emotional development. BPD is not a brain disease.

3. **Help those with BPD become aware** of the very defenses in place to protect them from pain. That pain itself must be understood. Understanding is a journey to reunite with the dissociated inner child—to find the lost, authentic self in order to learn to self-soothe and self-validate, and to learn through a wide scope of modalities and methods. Feelings can be unlearned. Different choices can be made.

Essentially, we must humanize the experience of those who end up with what I think is a poorly defined diagnosis—a diagnosis that focuses on symptoms rather than the experience of those in a great deal of pain, particularly those who need help navigating their early childhood experiences, wounds, and trauma (in many cases) to find and know the "self" lost to abandonment.

Object relations theorist Melanie Klein pioneered the identification of the effects of the central causation of BPD. Klein is quoted as having said that early childhood (perceived or actual physical and/or emotional) abandonment causes "the psychological death of the otherwise burgeoning authentic self." She also talks about the "anxiety of the death extinct." Humanizing what this experience has entailed for those diagnosed with BPD, and helping each client understand what this means in their own life, is the key vehicle through which a host of psychological defense mechanisms has thrived. These defense mechanisms have blocked the very awareness that, once one comes to understand and work through and beyond, creates the process and the road to recovery from BPD.

Professionals need to approach each client where they are. Engage them in a real, therapeutic relationship—one that supports client retention long enough for clients to trust the process and persevere.

A. J. Mahari lives in Ontario, Canada. She is a professional counselor, writer, and Life/BPD/Loved Ones Coach. She has the voice of a consumer expert. Her knowledge comes from firsthand life experience in the trenches of BPD and her choices to get well and stay well. A. J. has left the valleys of mental illness behind and has climbed the many mountains of her past in order to recover from BPD, while learning to thrive in her life as someone with Asperger's syndrome.

Her prolific presence on the Internet includes numerous articles, blog posts, her BPD Inside Out podcast, and YouTube videos. She has written and published over 20 e-books and over 35 audio programs. Visit her online at ajmahari.ca.

Hitting Rock Bottom

By Cori Magnotta

Lying in the hospital at the age of 21 after heart failure caused by anorexic and bulimic behaviors should have been my rock bottom. But, unfortunately, the real rock bottom was being arrested and almost going to jail for my desperate need to be liked, praised, and accepted.

My parents are as toxic as they come. I never had my own identity; I was always "Cindy's daughter." My mother's constant attempts to make our lives seem perfect and hide family secrets sent one message loud and clear: "You are not good enough the way you are."

I was a beauty queen, had a 4.0 GPA, and was a successful teenage model. None of it was ever good enough. A member of our church molested me when I was 8 years old. My mostly absent father told me I was "supposed to be a boy" every chance he got. When I was 14, it came out that he had been having an affair with another woman my entire life. As an only child, it became my job to console my morbidly obese mother. We were already completely enmeshed, but in my teenage years, our relationship reached a new level of dysfunction.

I wasn't allowed to do anything on my own. When I spoke to friends on the phone, my mother would sit on another phone line silently and script what I was to say next. In high school, she would spend hours online typing to my friends, pretending to be me. She would later print out these conversations so I could read what *I* had said and not look foolish to my friends in school the next day.

The real assault came when I began a relationship with Andy, my high school sweetheart who became my husband. My mother would type sexually explicit things to him all night, despite my pleading with her to stop. I frequently attempted to sabotage my relationship with him just to put an end to the embarrassment, confusion, and humiliation I felt with my mother running my life. My mother frequently did my homework for me saying I wasn't "good enough" to do it and I would "just screw it up anyway." It was as though I was a marionette and she was the puppet master.

T. J. (see page 33) also described feeling like a "puppet," being easily manipulated but lacking the strength to immediately break free from the puppet master's hand. Can you relate to this experience?

Andy was a grade above me in school. When he left for college six hours away, my mother was truly in control in our relationship. During one of our visits, I tried to break up with him, saying I didn't trust him being over 400 miles away and that I knew he would cheat on me. He said, "I would never do that; why would you even think that?" Everything came pouring out, I told him about my father's

On the surface I had it all put together; I was an attractive blonde with a ton of friends and had recently won the title of Miss Connecticut Teen. But nothing could have been further from the truth.

affair, my eating disorder, and that he had really been talking to my mother online, not me. We started sending e-mails instead of using AOL Instant Messenger to talk to each other.

One morning, my mother checked my email. She saw our conversations and went absolutely ballistic. She exclaimed, "Blood isn't thicker than water in this family!" She chased me around the house throwing things, breaking objects, and hitting me.

I jumped into my car and drove to school as fast as I could, crying hysterically the entire way. I ran directly to the crisis intervention counselor's office and told her what had happened that morning. I spent hours sobbing through my story, a secret life I kept hidden from everyone.

On the surface I had it all put together; I was an attractive blonde with a ton of friends and had recently won the title of Miss Connecticut Teen. But nothing could have been further from the truth. I was an emotional mess, addicted to laxatives and diet pills (both forced down my throat from the age of 11). I remember the crisis intervention counselor saying to me, "If you weren't about to turn 18, I would call the Department of Children's Services for you. What you are experiencing is abuse. Go to college, go directly to the counseling center, and get the help you need. It will be a long road, but you can do it." I had no idea of just how long that road was going to be.

The following year, I followed Andy to college at Rochester Institute of Technology (RIT). I was a social work major. I was determined to save the world, to work with teenagers, and to empower people to overcome the challenges I had overcome as well. It didn't exactly go as planned. My first semester, I achieved a 4.0 GPA and worked as hard as I always had to gain approval and acceptance. I continued to starve myself because there was so little I had been able to control in my life. My mother frequently made me feel guilty for "abandoning her." While my "sin" had been growing up and going to college—something normal children do—my mother made it out to be a heinous crime. She frequently made the six-hour trip to RIT and would follow me around campus without my knowledge. She'd ask friends about me. She'd go to campus security saying I was missing and demanding my whereabouts.

I had gone to the counseling center upon arriving at college. My counselor worked with me on how to communicate with my mother. I discussed my eating disorder, as well as my need to please everyone around me and gain acceptance. She immediately caught and noted a few obvious behaviors I had never noticed before: I never stopped smiling, no matter what horrible feeling I was discussing; I would say "you" when referring to myself; and I seemed to view things in only all-or-nothing extremes. Either I earned an A or I withdrew from the class. I either starved myself completely or binged on everything in sight.

After one particularly awful encounter with my mother, I overdosed on NyQuil. I just couldn't deal with all of the conflicting emotions and wanted to dull the pain. I was always on an emotional roller coaster, jumping from emotion to emotion and not understanding any of it.

Andy and I decided to get married at the end of my freshman year of college. He had been my rock for five years at that point and accepted every part of me: the good, the bad, and the ugly. My mother hated the idea of me getting married and would frequently have outbursts. One day, when we were on an errand to pick up my veil, I said something that upset her. She pulled the car over and kicked me out on the highway. I stood on the side of a major highway crying and scared (this was before the days of cell phones). She eventually came back around to get me, lecturing me on how lucky I was that she returned. If I were truly lucky, a police officer would have come by and seen a 19-year-old abandoned on the side of a major highway!

My mother absolutely ruined my wedding day—something I will never forgive her for and still get angry about nearly 15 years later. I was over an hour late to my own wedding. On the morning of, she cursed me, saying "I curse you to have only one daughter, to give that daughter everything, do everything for her, and then she leaves you." (I'm very happy to say God has blessed me with a little boy so far.) Then, she refused to get into the limousine, claiming she was going to physically die that day. Finally, she refused to be in the wedding photos. I have one photo of her at my wedding; she is screaming at me as others look on.

At the end of my junior year of college, the social work department delivered shocking news: The department was closing. With the school mostly focused on technology, the social work department wasn't strong, so the college decided it was no longer worth supporting. I was devastated. My favorite professors—people who I had become very much attached to—left for other teaching positions. Because I had dropped so many classes over the years, I was behind. It was becoming obvious I wasn't going to graduate from the program. My mother also stopped supporting me financially—and I needed money.

I longed for the attention that modeling and pageants had once brought me. Seeking drama, approval, and financial stability, I started stripping at the local strip club. I knew that my father had frequented strip clubs, and I got a "high" off of being the woman that married men would stare at while their wives and children were at home.

Being a stripper meant needing to be thin, so I began ordering diet pills online, taking laxatives by the fistful, and starving myself. After four months of this behavior, my body gave out. I was rushed to the hospital with heart failure caused by my eating disorder. The day after I was admitted to the hospital, a therapist came to discuss what had happened. After talking about the extremes in my life, she asked me if I had heard of borderline personality disorder. I told her that I had, but that I only had an eating disorder, not a personality disorder. I was referred to a mental health center and treated for my eating disorder. At the suggestion of my therapist, I obtained a position at a four-star hotel as a front desk agent. I instantly fell in love with hospitality.

After my husband graduated from college, we returned home to Connecticut. I bounced around several different hospitality positions, constantly convinced that life was better at another hotel. I still had very inappropriate reactions and emotions to situations. I would cry at the drop of a hat and was unable to handle it if I disappointed someone. I saw one therapist who requested the files from my previous therapists; all of them mentioned a suspicion that I was a "high-functioning borderline."

It took me eight years to go from front desk agent to hotel general manager, the highest position one can hold at a hotel on the property level. I was desperate for approval from my employees, guests of the hotel, and my supervisors. I did many things that can be viewed as

Therapy is not easy or for the faint of heart.

manipulative and dishonest, all from a place of seeking the approval and praise I didn't receive as a child.

One of those things was making a fake rewards account, using it to obtain gift cards and items for the hotel that were not in the budget. I would give the gift cards away to guests and employees in attempt to "buy" their approval. I personally paid hotel invoices with my own money to make it seem like I was managing the hotel better than I actually was.

One day, my supervisor made inappropriate sexual advances toward me. When I rejected him and threatened to report him, he said, "You better hope you've done nothing wrong or you'll be sorry." Once audited, my schemes became apparent. I was arrested and formally charged with embezzlement and fraud.

Arrested. I had never even received a single detention in my 12 years of school. My "disease to please" had hit a new level of repercussions. I didn't personally profit a single cent from my theft, but I was sure about to pay with my reputation, sanity, and money. My entire life, I thrived on being the nicest—the person who could fix anything for anyone who came my way. I usually "fixed" things at my own expense—and I was about to pay for it big time.

The most difficult part was realizing that none of the people I bent over backward for were there for me in my time of need. The employee I gave petty cash to for gas money kicked me when I was down, stating she witnessed me misappropriating funds. The sales manager I gave gift cards to so she could reward clients sold me out as fast as possible. Ironically, the people I hadn't done anything for, or ever given anything to, were the people who stood by me when I needed friendship and support the most.

> *Through Cori's experience, we better understand BPD as a roller coaster, with several ups and downs on the path to, during, and even after treatment. What personal highs and lows have you endured?*

After spending nearly a decade after college building my hospitality career, in a day it was over. I was severely depressed. It quickly became very apparent that I had attracted all of the wrong people into my life. I realized that there was a definite destructive pattern and I needed to stop these behaviors before I ended up completely destroying myself. I found a psychiatrist at the Institute of Living in Hartford, Connecticut, who specialized in treating borderline personality disorder. I also found a lawyer who listened to my entire story and gave me her word that I was not going to be the same person who walked into this storm—and that was going to be a good thing.

I began working on myself like never before, mostly because I had never truly worked on myself. I'd always gone through the motions in therapy: filled out the food journals, smiled, and told my therapist I was fine and making progress. This therapist was different—beyond different.

During our first session, I sat opposite him, smiling as I recounted everything I had been through. He sat quietly for a moment. Then, he responded with a racial slur and I sat there, dumbfounded. What had he just called me? He explained that I was so polite in smiling as I recounted my horrors that I must be a slave to my emotions and to the desperate approval I sought from others.

In the months and years that followed, I worked diligently to overcome my insecurities and find my true authentic self. Therapy is not easy or for the faint of heart. There is a lot of pain involved in holding up a mirror to the most painful parts of yourself and chipping away at the parts deemed "ugly." I still struggle. That amazing psychiatrist retired last year at the age of 77. There's nothing easy about having borderline, but there's a bit of good and beauty in every situation.

Cori Magnotta is an advocate for stopping the stigma of mental illness, and an official resource liason for the National Association of Anorexia Nervosa and Associated Disorders. She has been married to her high school sweetheart for 15 years and has an infant son. She strongly believes that there is always hope, help, and healing from mental illness.

In Sickness and in Health

By Darren and Kate

Darren and Kate are married and have been dealing with the reality of borderline personality disorder for many years. What follows is a candid conversation about how it feels to be impacted by BPD—from the vantage points of both a person diagnosed and a person working to support an individual with BPD.

Kate: What did it feel like growing up? I know you always felt there was something different about you, and it was frustrating.

Darren: I always knew I was different from a very early age—always being told I was "oversensitive" and "always taking things to heart," but the emotions I felt were so intense. I guess I was sensitive. From the age of about 12, I started harming myself, especially when I felt rejected or feared abandonment, and would pretend I walked into a door or cut myself accidentally to hide what I was doing. By 15, I was starting to get into trouble with the police, experimenting with drugs and alcohol, and was trying desperately to fit in to different groups.

I constantly have to think about what or how I say things
to you, while also trying to understand that it's okay for you
to express yourself.

I was first hospitalized in 2002, again in 2008, and in 2014 when
I finally received a diagnosis. I'd spent 20 years on different types of
antidepressants. Doctors were treating me for depression. I knew it
was not just depression, but I had no idea what else it was. How did
you feel before my diagnosis?

Kate: Even though you had not been diagnosed, you were completely
honest from the beginning of our relationship about your mental
health problems. I had never had any dealings with mental illness
before and was pretty naïve in the beginning. I never once thought
about running. In my eyes, I had found this man I was crazy about.
You made me feel safe, protected, happy, and loved. I was warned
by others to stay away, but I'd rather make my own mind up about
a person. I believed it was worth finding out more about you. When
you were finally diagnosed, I remember feeling relieved and quite
positive. It felt like, "Yes! We can finally get him the correct help!
We can do our own research of ways to make his life easier to cope
with." It definitely helped to have a name for your struggles and be
able to learn how I could help. What did it mean to you to finally have
a proper diagnosis?

Darren: I was in a psychiatric hospital in 2008. It was then I was
originally diagnosed with antisocial personality disorder and an anxiety disorder. I'd never heard of a personality disorder before, so when
I was released after a short while, I came home and looked it up

on the Internet. I was amazed at what I was reading. Most things seemed to ring true, but not all of it. It was then that I came across borderline personality disorder and instantly related to all the criteria to meet the diagnosis. My psychiatrist from the community mental health team then diagnosed me with BPD—or, more suitably, emotionally unstable personality disorder. it came as such a huge relief to realize suddenly that I'm not alone in this struggle and it actually had a name. I couldn't believe what I was reading; it could have been written about me personally.

Receiving the diagnosis felt liberating. Finally, after all those years knowing there was something seriously wrong, I didn't feel so alone. Somebody out there understood exactly what I was going through—in fact, there were millions. Why had I never heard of such an illness when it seems so common?

I started to do my own research on BPD and everywhere I looked they were talking about *me*! My erratic and intense mood swings, suicidal ideation, impulsiveness, identity disturbances, instability, self-harm, dissociation, a history of substance and alcohol abuse, guilt, shame, unstable relationships, black-and-white thinking, and a great fear of rejection and abandonment. This is me! With it all finally outlined more clearly for me, I began to wonder: What is it like to live with me?

Kate: I personally live every day with fear and worry. "Walking on eggshells" is a perfect phrase to explain exactly how I often feel as I walk through life. I am always worried about causing an episode. One thing you have to understand is that everything I say is taken literally and usually blown completely out of context by you. I constantly have to think about what or how I say things to you, while also trying to understand that it's okay for you to express yourself. What does it feel like having BPD?

I never know who or what I'm going to be in 10 minutes' time.
I question who I am and what my values are all the time.

Darren: Living with BPD is nothing short of hell when I'm not feeling good. Emotions are amplified. I can feel multiple emotions
simultaneously, but not really know what or how I am feeling at the
same time. I tend to see things in black-and-white terms; everything
is either great or really awful. I have intrusive thoughts of suicide,
murder, self-criticism, and feelings of being empty, hopeless, and
worthless. When I'm feeling bad, I ruminate over all the failures and
bad times I've been through. I am prone to outbursts of inappropriate anger and rage—rage that is usually bottled up and turned
inward. As you well know, I use unhealthy coping mechanisms, like
self-harm, overdosing, self-medicating, and so on.

*Darren and Kate have gotten to a place where they are able to
candidly discuss Darren's struggles with BPD, and the effect
it has on their relationship. Whether you yourself contend
with BPD, or your loved one—whether it is a spouse, child, or
parent, consider having a similar conversation so you can fully
understand where the other is coming from.*

I can be really happy one moment, but within minutes that can
change for no apparent reason. Certain trivial events can trigger my
BPD behaviors. I never know who or what I'm going to be in 10 minutes' time. I question who I am and what my values are all the time.

When I get overwhelmed, I tend to dissociate and lose touch with reality; when people talk to me, it is comparable to a radio playing in the background. I can hear noises but cannot hear them properly. My emotions are a constant roller coaster that is exhausting and draining. I misinterpret things and how they are said, as well as body language and facial expressions.

I go to bed tired and wake up tired. When I get extremely tired, I hear critical voices inside of my head telling me I'm a bad person and I should do terrible things, like harm others or myself. They tell me I'm useless and people would be better off without me. Moods can change so quickly; happiness turns to sadness, courage to fear, positivity to anxiety, and hope to hopelessness. Even when I am happy, I feel a sense of guilt that I shouldn't be happy. I sometimes sabotage my own happiness. I am impulsive and often do things I regret instantly. I overthink everything and ruminate on mistakes I've made in the past. I sometimes feel like a fraud because I don't really know who I am and often take on the persona of the person I'm with at the time.

I can feel like a monster due to some of the terrible thoughts I have. Although they are only thoughts, they can be very extreme and shocking. I'm terrified of being abandoned by my loved ones. I worry all the time that I am a bad parent and look for reasons to reinforce this. I often feel childlike with my emotions and find it embarrassing when I can think clearly. I don't feel deserving of love or kindness and wonder how anyone could love me. Sometimes I feel that everybody hates me, and I often hate myself.

Kate: I know it's a daily struggle that we have dealt with for years. Tell me, when you're feeling upset, what is the worst way I can respond to you?

Darren: This is very difficult for me to answer. Sometimes I want to be left alone, but at the same time I don't want to be ignored; this makes me feel more isolated and alone.

The usual phrases of "Come on, not this again?" and "Why are you being like this?" are probably the least helpful. I really, really don't want to feel this way, and if I could just change it, I would. Also, to dismiss my feelings as "You're just being silly," is a big fat no. How do you perceive me as a parent?

Kate: I truly believe you are a good dad—if I didn't, I would not have our kids in this environment. You can be frustrating at times. When you are having an episode you can become very withdrawn, and this is when I can feel like a single parent. In these times, I sometimes feel I have to do everything and this can be very stressful. You can switch off from the children and unknowingly ignore them. I just explain to them that you are having a "bad head" day, and they seem to respond to this quite well and don't seem to take it personally. I feel you focus too much on all the negative stuff rather than all the positive stuff you do for them. Even though sometimes I have to force you to do stuff with us, you usually do it and this is something I think you should be proud of. How do you perceive yourself as a parent?

Darren: I always tend to focus on the negative to reaffirm that I am a bad dad. I love and cherish my children so much that I try to hide as much as I can from them because I'm scared of passing it on to them. I do feel like a grumpy dad a lot. I am often so wrapped up in my own thoughts that I become a bit distant. I look at other dads and feel jealous of them; they don't seem to be struggling. I also miss out on a lot of fun family times because I'm wrapped up in an unwanted thought or emotion. Having said that, I am very protective of my children and would never let anyone or anything harm them.

Kate: How can I tell when you are struggling?

Darren: My silence is usually my loudest scream. When I push you away is when I usually need you closest. I have difficulty asking for help and feel like you should just know I'm feeling low, suicidal, or whatever. I often think people should read my mind rather than having to ask for help. I may be extra tired all the time, have trouble sleeping, or appear vacant and uninterested in anything. It's difficult to tell someone you love that you are struggling, as it can be taken personally. What is the worst bit about living with my BPD for you?

Kate: The thought of suicide is unbearable. You are impulsive and this is the worst part for me to understand; you just don't think of or see the consequences of your actions. This gives me feelings of desperation, hopelessness, fear, anger, and worry. I must have been through the scenario of telling our children hundreds of times that their daddy's not ever coming home, how I would have to explain it's not their fault. I imagine having to somehow try to comfort them through it all, from the funeral to getting them back to school; the whole scenario plays out in my head and makes me fearful and anxious.

It's very difficult at times to deal with these feelings.

Darren: Do you see anything as positive aspects of BPD?

Kate: You love with your entire heart. Even though emotions are really difficult for you to deal with, you do have them, which is a very positive part of your personality. You are also very intelligent, and I can listen to your knowledge of life or the world for hours. Yes, you have BPD, but as a person you will not let this destroy you. Instead, I have seen you go out there and find out as much as you can and get as much help as possible, and this is something I greatly admire about you. What have you done and found most helpful to help yourself deal with BPD?

What do you admire most about yourself or the person in your life with BPD?

Darren: I have sought all the help I can get. I have had one-to-one psychotherapy, which, due to circumstances out of my control, was cut short. I have completed two anger-management courses and a "living with emotion" course. I attend a support group one day per week that has been the most helpful thing to date. We cover all kinds of life skills related to BPD. It also gives me the chance to mix with and share experiences with other people with BPD. I practice mindfulness meditation, which I find helpful to an extent and is something I want to explore further.

Kate: What medications have you found that work for you?

Darren: Over the years, I've been on a wide range of medications: antidepressants, mood stabilizers, antipsychotics, tranquilizers, and sleep medication. All of these drugs have offered relief from some of the symptoms, but there is no magic pill for BPD. I currently take antidepressants, mood stabilizers, and antianxiety medication, which I have found the most helpful so far. What would you say to anyone living with a person with BPD?

Kate: Unless you live with someone who has BPD, it is hard to understand the constant thoughts and worries that go through my mind. Four suicide attempts is four too many. I try, and am as open and honest as I can be with our children, to reassure them that it's not their fault if daddy is angry or sad or disconnected. Our children, five and nine years old, know their daddy sometimes has a "bad head." I believe it's important for them to grow up knowing; this way it is more normal for them and they will have a better understanding and know they are not to blame. I have read books with my eldest son about depression. We have looked at pictures of the brain, and we have discussed different emotions, and how it is okay to have emotions and express your feelings.

I have two really proud moments regarding this. First, is hearing him talking to his cousin about the dangers of touching medication that doesn't belong to you. Second, his schoolteacher told me she overheard him telling a friend not to be nasty to an autistic child because not all our brains work in the same way. These things made me glad and made me feel we were right to educate him about mental illness. So I'd definitely tell others to work on education, and not hiding their struggles, whether it's with their children, family, or friends.

It's definitely not easy living with someone with BPD, but it's worth all the heartache for the many happy memories we have and continue to make together. I also feel you have made me a better person and taught me that mental illness should not be swept under the carpet or considered a taboo subject.

Darren and Kate have been together for 15 years and married for 10. Darren suffers from BPD. Kate works as a removals administrator, while Darren works to recover from his illness and raise awareness for the disorder.

A View of Therapy from Therapist and Patient Perspectives

By Nina and Samantha

Nina, the therapist, and Samantha, the client, are the two halves of a counseling relationship. In the following pages, Nina and Samantha share a candid discussion about what it's like being on either end of that relationship.

What Was Therapy Like When You Two Began?

Samantha: I remember being drained. I would come home and sleep for two hours afterward. Therapy was very difficult in the beginning. I had just been hospitalized, and my former therapist was not working out for me anymore. I felt vulnerable, to say the least. I felt afraid to start all over again with a new therapist, yet I knew I needed help. I was also grateful to have a therapist who would take me on despite my difficult history.

Nina: When I agreed to work with Samantha, I had heard about her difficult history and thought, "I really want to make a difference for her." I had recently finished an intensive training in DBT and felt a responsibility to use my training to help someone who so desperately needed this treatment.

Samantha: At first, although I felt Nina's compassion, it was hard for me to believe that someone truly cared. Now, though, I genuinely feel her compassion and can appreciate it as well.

Nina: What stands out most in my mind is the day after our first session. Samantha called me for phone coaching. Samantha agreed to try my suggestions and I had thought the coaching had gone well, until it was time to end the call. All of a sudden, Samantha started escalating: sobbing and telling me how much pain she was in and how she couldn't stand it. Well, I realized very quickly that I had better figure out a way to validate and support Samantha and at the same time give her a way to manage her emotions without me. This beginning basically set the stage for most of our work together. Samantha has moved from expecting me to "save her," to understanding that she can actually save herself.

Can You Say More about Your Treatment Methods?

Nina: DBT was designed for someone like Samantha, someone who has been diagnosed with BPD and PTSD from her childhood abuse. Her multiple attempts at suicide, 22 hospitalizations, and having burned out previous therapists signaled that she absolutely needed DBT, the gold standard treatment for her conditions and behaviors. We followed the standard DBT protocol: Samantha came to me for individual therapy once a week while attending a DBT skills group led by a different therapist on our DBT team. We used between-session phone coaching to support her using DBT skills during difficult moments, and I went to our DBT team weekly meeting to make sure that I was staying adherent to the treatment and holding my limits so that I would not burn out.

Samantha: Nina uses a variety of methods. She definitely has her hands full when it comes to me! It cannot be easy to deal with someone who is so high risk and very needy. What stands out for me is the open communication that she has with me, her use of the DBT skills when dealing with me in general—specifically, how she encourages me with positive reinforcement and teaches me how to be dialectical, mindful, and use my wise mind. The validation I receive from her really builds me into a stronger person, knowing that I am worthwhile in someone's eyes. Her calm manner helps me relax in her presence. She structures our sessions well, yet she is not rigid. She points out my distorted and judgmental thinking in a compassionate and caring manner. She listens well and reflects on what I have shared. She is detail-oriented, and aware of my patterns in thoughts and behaviors.

Many of the contributors in this book have had unfortunate experiences with therapists and the therapy process, especially in the early phases of diagnosis. When searching for a therapist, it's important to have candid conversations, as Nina and Samantha had done. A poorly matched patient and therapist can lead to disastrous outcomes, particularly when dealing with sensitive mental health issues.

What's Helpful for Samantha as a Patient?

Samantha: I find it very helpful when Nina validates me, and when she uses compassionate words because I always try to mind-read and I am usually wrong. I also have a hard time with eye contact, so when I hear those comforting words—despite the fact that I cannot read her facial expressions—it is a balm to my hurting soul. I appreciate that she respects my boundaries, keeps confidentiality, is open to change, and respects me as a person; she sees past my behaviors and skewed thinking. I feel that she believes in me and gives me space to share my emotions, yet without forcing me at all. I find it helpful that she is open to coaching me, and her genuine caring is making me tear up as I say this. I feel that she has given me a new lease on life. She is encouraging and uses dialectics in order to help me out of the "stuck" place I feel I am in many times. She is the only one who believes I have a future. She does not shame me or put me down, sees me for who I am, and accepts me as I am now.

Nina: What's so interesting for me is that, if I'd answered first, I would have said what was most helpful for Samantha is that while I understand that because of the pain of her childhood and present she sees suicide as her only way out, that she can instead use her DBT skills to build herself a life without suffering—a life even with satisfaction and self-worth. And because I never gave up on her, I've pushed her to take the next step, and once accomplished, the next. Sometimes she gets mad at me, calls me a brat, and tells me she's not interested in using skills. But I believe that because I don't give up, while at the same time validating how difficult it is and how invalidating it feels to be told to use your skills (as if it's so easy), she knows someone believes in her. This helps her be willing to try to believe in herself and to work to change.

I guess that translates to what she said: She feels that I understand her suffering, respect her, and believe in her ability to change and build a future.

What Behaviors Were or Weren't Helpful for You as the Therapist to Work with, Nina?

Nina: Samantha's frequent emergency phone calls—or "save me" calls, as we nicknamed them—really motivated me to be effective. For me, the turning point was when Samantha called me at 4 a.m. and croaked out that she had a tie around her neck, could barely breathe, and couldn't get it off. I told her that I was going to hang up and call her cousin whom she lived with. Samantha said, "Wait, I think I can get it off . . . Yes, it's off. I'm OK." Frankly, I got really

By knowing which behaviors had to be addressed first, we were able to carve out a path leading out of the chaos.

angry, even as I knew that although I felt manipulated into speaking to her in the middle of the night when I was asleep, Samantha didn't mean to manipulate me. At the same time, I knew that if these crises didn't stop, I would burn out, which I didn't want to do. The event galvanized me to set firm limits to what behaviors I could no longer tolerate. Not because I was angry but because I was concerned that therapy was not working. I told Samantha that I could not keep treating her if what I was giving her was not enough to stop her suicidal tendencies: She needed to be safe. Happily, this limit helped motivate Samantha to use her DBT skills. And using skills is helping her become more in control and to experience more satisfying moments.

In terms of the therapy as a whole, sticking to DBT's hierarchy of target behaviors was essential. Samantha often came in with more than one crisis each session: financial difficulties, having lost her financial aid for college, being asked to leave her cousin's house every holiday so that her cousin's married children and grandchildren could stay instead, and a run-in with her brother who had abused her for 10 years are some examples. In the beginning especially, she became extremely emotionally dysregulated and wanted to escape her intense suffering by overdosing, being hospitalized, or self-harming. DBT protocol was our lifesaver and compass. By knowing which behaviors had to be addressed first, we were able to carve out a path leading out of the chaos. At the beginning of each session, we would make an agenda so that while we were prioritizing working on Samantha's suicidality, hospitalizations, and self-harm, we also left time for the present issue and how she could use her skills to manage that as well. Paradoxically, by starting with a Behavior Chain Analysis (a DBT worksheet we use to help someone understand why they're behaving in a certain way) of an episode of an intense urge to overdose, we were able to weave in many of her daily stressors to the discussion, seeing how they were all related. And we were able to then discuss ways to use her DBT skills to manage both. Her willingness to work with the structure and incorporate skills was what helped me as the therapist. Her advancements encouraged me that we were being successful.

Can You Offer Any Insight into What You've Learned?

Samantha: Stick with the therapy despite the difficulty, as it is well worth it. Therapists who are not completely trained in DBT will not understand you fully; stick with those who are well trained. Come prepared to each meeting with notes as to what you want to discuss. In session you can choose to disclose it or not, but come prepared. Confront therapists and ask for clarification when necessary. Treat your therapist with respect, as they very likely have been through a difficult journey. Most of all, respect yourself, as you are brave and daring to expose the darkest places of your heart.

Nina: The incredible importance of using dialectics: always shifting between accepting the client as she is and feeling with her, but at the same time, encouraging, even seemingly demanding, the use of skills and the setting and maintaining of my own limits. I've also learned the importance of collaboration between a client and her

Treat your therapist with respect, as they very likely have been through a difficult journey. Most of all, respect yourself, as you are brave and daring to expose the darkest places of your heart.

therapist. By contributing my therapeutic skills, keeping the focus on our goals during the sessions, and showing my validation and empathy for her struggle, Samantha was able to do her part of working hard to change her reactions and thoughts to effectively manage her emotions and build the life she wants. She also found her own voice in our work, expressing her needs and the inner demons we needed to deal with in order to accomplish our goals. I feel extremely honored to participate in Samantha's struggle and growth, and to have learned so much from our work together.

Samantha was diagnosed with BPD when she was 18. Ten years later, she has exceeded her wildest expectations and has enrolled in graduate school. She never would have believed that there is a light at the end of the tunnel and knows now that change can and will happen. Her biggest message to others is, "Take hope!"

Nina Kaweblum, LCSW, MA, M.Ed. is a DBT therapist, intensively trained by Behavior Tech and awaiting approval for certification. Nina is a founding member of DBT LifeSkills, a private group practice dedicated to helping clients reduce their suffering and build a better life. She works individually with adolescents and adults and runs standard, multifamily, and advanced DBT skills classes.

Working with Mindfulness

By Susan T. Lindau

On Being a Patient

I often say finding the right therapist is like looking for the right pair of shoes. You want a style that is right for you, and you want a good fit—something you can wear for hours at a time. In looking for a therapist, search for someone with whom you feel comfortable and who has the skill and training to support you in learning how to manage your psychic pain.

My own experience of looking for that comfortable fit led me through meetings that, in retrospect, are pretty funny. At the time, though, they left me confused, wondering if it would ever be possible to find help.

There was the therapist who seemed kind and professional at first, but told me she could never work with me because my history was too overwhelming for her—and she couldn't help place me with another therapist! Imagine how hopeless I felt after that meeting.

> Susan offers a unique perspective as someone who was a
> patient before she was a therapist. How might one inform
> the other?

Then there was the therapist who, during our first meeting, insisted I reveal everything about my traumatic history. I told her that I had already covered those issues and wanted to work on the present. She insisted that we could not work on the present without exploring that past. Evidently, she wasn't listening to me, her client.

The right therapist is a combination: a supportive parent, an understanding friend, and a professional who can project these qualities within their ability to communicate clear guidelines for the work together. Often, clients enter therapy without an understanding of how therapy works or what to expect. Even people who have previously been to therapy and have worked with another professional can stumble when trying to find the right counselor. It can be difficult to know what to ask and what to look for.

There are resources available. Visit *Psychology Today* (psychologytoday.com) and search the listings of therapists in your area. As a potential client, it's especially important to review the methods your therapist uses to treat clients, their training credentials, and the insurance plans their clinic accepts. The National Association of Social Workers (socialworkers.org) maintains a directory of qualified therapists. The best source in my mind is the Association for Behavior and Cognitive Therapy (abct.org), which has a list of therapists trained in various forms of cognitive behavioral therapy (CBT), a crucial method for treating BPD.

Don't be ambivalent or afraid to ask a friend or family member for a referral. You might ask yourself, "Do I want my friend to know I'm looking for a therapist?" or "Will they judge me?" These are legitimate questions, but don't let them get in the way of getting the support that's so essential to managing BPD. Your friend may have a counselor they like and are eager to recommend. While everyone's different, it may be an appropriate recommendation if your friend is comfortable with that clinician.

When approaching a potential new therapist, it's important to ask, "Are you the therapist for me?" Many people don't feel comfortable asking such a direct question, but it's necessary before diving into the therapeutic process. You have to approach your therapist with positive feelings. It can be difficult for patients to know what other questions to ask, such as what approaches they use, what they think the goal of therapy is, and what is expected of the patient.

BPD is difficult to live with—even more so if you're not engaged in therapy. It can be frustrating, and you may go through a few therapists before finding the right one. I assure you—it will be worthwhile in the end.

On Being a Therapist

I've gone from being a patient to being a treating professional, a move that's allowed me to deeply understand both where patients are coming from, and the difficulties they face before, during, and after treatment. From the nervousness of a first visit to facing issues in session that you'd rather not address, therapy can be a confusing process. When a potential client contacts me, I know this initial exchange is as important as my academic credentials and experience. While that first contact may not provide much information, the manner in which a therapist finds time to meet with a potential client is an indication of their flexibility. Small things, like providing information about parking and traffic, express any clinician's understanding of the obstacles patients manage just to get to the office and serve to make a patient more optimistic about the potential for a good connection.

If you have BPD, you've probably been turned away from therapy, as I was, given that many therapists believe that patients with BPD are notoriously difficult to treat. And I'll be honest, some of my BPD clients occasionally make me wonder why I agreed to work with them—like Mary Beth, who claims to have every immune system disorder known to man, or Aziz, who no one in his family will speak to.

Think back to your first forays into therapy. What did you appreciate from your therapist? What wasn't helpful?

But Aziz is pleasant and charming when he is not spewing venom against any perceived personal insult, and Mary Beth has demonstrated a sweet capacity to understand parenting skills. And then I wonder what prevents her from providing the same love for herself. Therein rests the challenge of working with people struggling with BPD. Many individuals, not just the ones I see regularly, have challenges that make it hard to get through the day. My clients, on the other hand, suffer from enormous fear, anger, and sadness. BPD has been described as being so painful that it hurts as much as third-degree burns. With this knowledge, I must remind myself that they have asked for instructions for getting out of their own hell.

It does happen! Through patience and consistency on my part and committed hard work by the clients, they are able to break free of their emotional prison. What did Anna do to move from the just-fired administrative assistant to the completion of her master's degree to being currently employed in her chosen profession? It wasn't an easy or smooth path, and there were those predictable times when I wasn't sure I could hang in for another late evening call telling me she "just couldn't go on."

Anna is not unusual, and while the steps she took can be described here, it's helpful to understand what I used to move both of us to find inner peace: patience and consistency. Those two characteristics may be the best way to describe the environment in which I provided support. Often, I sound like a broken record. Reassuring clients again and again that, "Yes, it does feel awful. And you *can* make it."

While I am providing support to a client, I must tell myself over and over, it is their choice. I must stand aside and give them room to make their own mistakes. When Mary Beth wanted to take another job with a large corporation, I had to stand back and let her discover what was right for her. She chose to step away from the opportunity. Overtly, I supported her in a calm fashion. Internally, I was jumping up and down.

There were times when I was sure I'd never last through another session with Anna's sadness and reluctance to simply breathe. My own mindfulness practice is the key to my being able to continue to work with all the Annas and Mary Beths who come into my office. The two key skills I have learned that keep me coming into my office are mindfulness practice and the hard-learned skill of closing the

As I explain to these individuals who are suffering how the brain responds to fear or anger or sadness, I must model control of my own emotions.

door behind me at the end of the day. Once the client has gone home, it's time for me to take care of me.

Many people hear the word *mindful* or even the description of mindfulness and they get uncomfortable. My work is to educate the client. What is mindfulness? Has she had experience with sitting quietly and simply breathing? I often guide the client through a simple three-minute practice. Usually, the new client is surprised at how hard it is to quietly breathe through the instructions.

They hesitate to try the skill. Nothing has worked before. They have tried several types of therapy, medication, and even nontraditional forms of treatment. They know what CBT is and they have been exposed to group treatment, as well as traditional one-to-one psychodynamic support. Why should they feel better simply breathing? Clients come to me with horrible emotions that trigger dangerous and impulsive behaviors. I am willing to hospitalize them only as a last resort.

I make a simple request: Sit, breathe, and do not act on that powerful impulse to drive 90 miles an hour on the freeway, or take a handful of pills. The hard job for both the client and for me, the therapist, is to sit with the pain. Here is where I talk to them about what is happening neurobiologically, as the brain processes the enormous emotion. I must know enough about the way the brain processes emotions to inform the client in a calm manner that the pain does pass. They begin to understand that when this awful fear rises, the amygdala is firing and the portion of the brain that can make a choice based on facts—not feelings—is not online. It is important for me to explain to Anna or Mary Beth what is happening in their brain so that they can tolerate the 20 minutes it takes for this portion of the brain, the prefrontal cortex, to come online.

As I explain to these individuals who are suffering from their brain's response to fear or anger or sadness, I must model control of my own emotions. My own feelings are sometimes triggered by the experience of working with the patient who is so ambivalent about their ability to tolerate this pain. My work with these clients has forced me to recognize that supporting them requires conscious choices that both guide them and assist me. I am forced to recognize when I have done the work I can do for that session. We move to the place where we agree that they can take over living with this pain.

One of the requirements for coaching calls, those calls when the individual is in extreme pain and is not in the office, is to help the client choose the tools from skills training that will help in the immediate moment. This process of selecting that tool should not last longer than 10 minutes. The time limitation makes it possible for Anna or Mary Beth to think concisely and focus on the problem. Additionally, this restriction allows the therapist to provide concentrated support for 10 minutes, and to ensure that the individual and the therapist have found a tool for getting through those excruciating 20 minutes. Actual therapy is *not* provided during this call. The goal is to keep the client safe so that they can get treatment at the next session. And this activity all leads back to the basic tool of practicing mindfulness.

Mindfulness practices are not easy and yet, they are fundamentally the easiest tools I can practice for my own well-being. The difficult part of this tool is quieting the constant chatter in the brain and reaching the place where the noise in the brain slows requires regular and focused practice.

When thoughts of worry intrude, I go back to listening to my breath. Sometimes I add counting. When I get to 10, I start over again: Inhale, one; exhale one, inhale, two; exhale two; inhale, three, and so forth. The counting keeps me conscious, and the sound of the breath prevents my listening to the chatter in my brain.

When I began this practice, I found it easier to do a walking meditation: taking a breath with each single step. When that practice felt comfortable, I tried the hard (for me) practice of sitting. I began with the simple goal of quietly breathing for five minutes. After several years, I am beginning to feel that I have gotten a bit of skill at sitting quietly.

Breathe. It can make life more tolerable. Breathe. Connect with your own power to stay grounded and comfortable inside your skin.

Susan T. Lindau completed DBT intensive training in 2000. She first provided DBT to her clients at the LA County Department of Mental Health and now currently provides it in her private practice. She has continued to train through Behavioral Tech, most recently completing Advanced Training in DBT with Kelly Koerner and Charles Swenson, well-established experts in the field.

Hope for Recovery

By Michelle McFatridge

As I write this, I sit in palliative care, in a room dedicated to my father. He is dying and has a only few weeks left. It's devastating, but the family was prepared for this. The struggle with BPD on its own can be very difficult, but add a dying loved one to the mix and it's nearly unbearable. Getting myself out of bed each day is like pulling teeth. I wake up and wonder, "Is today the day?" But I still wake up, thank God, or whatever high power there may be, that I have another day with my daddy. Through my daily tears, I know that things will get better.

I remember my childhood very well. I was shy, I hated school, I lacked social skills, and I was very emotional and always had a difficult time trying to control my emotions. I was in and out of therapy a lot. I thought my doctors didn't know what they were talking about, how could they relate to what *I* was feeling?

At school, I was bullied a lot. I would regularly feign sickness on the regular just to have a reason to stay home. As I watched the bus leave my street, the sick feeling in my stomach immediately subsided

Mental illness had a stigma attached to it back then, it still
does. You didn't talk about it; you ignored and suppressed it.

because I knew I was safe for another day. Staying home in isolation
gave me solace. I didn't have to deal with anything, at least for a day.
As a child, I suffered from severe anxiety and clinical depression.
I was back and forth to the hospital for therapy following episodes
as severe as suicide attempts—it was hard on my poor mother and
father. They didn't know what to do.

> *Often, there's an assumption that BPD is the result of some*
> *sort of trauma, and can be traced back to an unstable*
> *childhood or other unfortunate circumstances. Reading*
> *Michelle's piece, we see this isn't always the case—BPD*
> *doesn't follow a fixed chain of events.*

Mental illness had a stigma attached to it back then, and it still
does. You didn't talk about it—you ignored and suppressed it. As a
family, we never discussed what was going on with me; it was swept
under the rug. Still, I was a good kid. I respected my parents and our
house rules. I never did anything illegal. I feared repercussion too
much to cause any trouble and was too anxious to risk breaking the
law. Even so, I was your stereotypical sister—stealing my older sister's clothing and fighting with my twin sister. I always felt that I had
it a bit harder than my sisters—I didn't feel equal in the treatment
we received. As far as I was concerned, they had it easy compared to
me. They didn't have the same struggles as me. Both were smart and

popular and had loads of friends. I had isolated myself and didn't share those characteristics.

Because of this, I was so excited when elementary school ended and I could start high school with a clean slate—no one would know me. Being bullied was over with (finally) and I'd make some new friends for once, maybe figure out who I really was. In high school, I excelled at everything I did. For the first two years, I did amazingly well; I was MVP at every sport I played, I was smart and had fairly decent marks, I even made a ton of friends. However, as time went on, I was back and forth to the hospital, again. Back on medications that I always took myself off of because, well, I didn't want to deal with society's ubiquitous stigma. "Take a pill to be happy? Not me, I don't need a pill to be happy! I could do this on my own, couldn't I?"

Fast-forward over a decade: I'm 30 years old. It's April of 2014. I'm in bed, sobbing my eyes out and I haven't gone to work in a month. I can't get out of bed. I can't stop crying. I can't eat. I was regularly lashing out in fits of anger towards my family for no reason whatsoever. I remember my mother rubbing my back and me sobbing, "I hate this feeling. I just want it to go away." That evening, my twin sister took me to the hospital. I met with my current psychiatrist (Dr. D.), who admitted me on the spot. I stayed in mental ward 2D for about a month. My medications were monitored closely, as was my sleep, my mood; the doctors paid close attention to anything that could help them help me recover.

One day. Dr. D. stopped by my room. He wanted to discuss my diagnosis.

"Diagnosis?" I thought I already knew what I had.

"You suffer from anxiety and depression, yes, but the big one is borderline personality disorder."

"Borderline, what?" I thought. "What the hell is he talking about? I don't have a disorder."

Dr. D. gave me a book to read, *Borderline Personality Disorder: An Information Guide for Families*. My concentration level was so bad at that point, even if I did manage to read it, I wasn't going to absorb any of it. I looked it over quickly, it was the least I could do. Things like, "What might have been a trivial slight to others was for me an emotional catastrophe," and "Highly sensitive to what's going on around them," were excerpts that stood out to me.

I had always had intense but short-lived bouts of anger, depression, and anxiety, but I didn't think it amounted to something bigger, something so severe. I knew I had a fear of abandonment, but I thought it was just one of those things that everyone felt from time to time. I thought it was just a quirk of mine, maybe a character flaw that I could work on. I didn't realize that these were the defining characteristics of a patient with BPD.

Dr. D. quickly put me on some new medication, which within days resulted in a significant difference in my mood. My anxiety was decreasing; my concentration was slowly returning. I could actually sit still for longer than a minute. It was soon after my specific combination of medication stabilized and proved effective that I was released from the hospital—but ironically, I didn't want out. I was comfortable in my little bubble, my space filled with people just like me. I didn't want to go out into that big scary world and have to face my demons and fears.

When the time came to inform my parents of my diagnosis, I was very anxious. I wasn't sure how they would react. I thought, "How are they going to treat me? What are they going to think of me?" I was so worried I was going to lose the support and love of my family that part of me didn't want my doctor to tell them. I had such a fear of abandonment, even though it was my family, who I knew loved me unconditionally.

My mother was in my room when my doctor came in. He explained my BPD diagnosis to her, and although she didn't have a clue what it was, she was so relieved to hear there was a reason behind my behavior. He gave her the same book he had given me to read, which helped my whole family understand my past and current behavior and learn a bit more about who I was and what having BPD meant. My family began reading and educating themselves on BPD and learning strategies for coping with me, especially during one of my "episodes."

What are some of your triggers?

Triggers are something that those with BPD, and their loved ones, should be well aware of. My twin sister is a huge trigger for me. She can be extremely difficult to deal with, although I know everything she does is out of love. Growing up, she sure knew how to push my buttons, but I know now that it was all out of frustration. I've talked to her about what it's like living with someone with BPD. She believes that when I am in one of my "episodes," I become extremely irrational and it's incredibly difficult to have a conversation with me because I become so defensive. From my perspective, having difficult conversations with me has always made me worry that people are preparing to leave me and no longer love or support me. My mother has always said it's incredibly difficult to be honest with me without me having to react negatively, whether by lashing out at the truth or isolating and removing myself from the situation at hand.

Each positive word we say to ourselves is pushing us forward, towards our recovery.

Through therapy, I have been working on these issues incredibly hard, through DBT, with my psychiatrist. Although there have been incredibly trying times, my family has been an incredible source of love and support. My mother has learned not to walk on eggshells around me and to be open and honest with me, at all costs. This doesn't help just me, but it helps her too. Living under that kind of stress, when you're walking on eggshells with someone, is never a healthy situation for either party. She speaks to me in a calm, loving manner and pushes me during the times I need to be pushed or just listens during the times I need a sounding board or shoulder to cry on. My relationship with my twin sister has also improved by leaps and bounds. I always felt attacked and judged when she would speak to me. It was incredibly frustrating, and I felt that I could never open up to her about anything. Now, she speaks to me softly and positively. She asks questions and asks how she can help. She comes with me to my therapy appointments so she's able to learn coping mechanisms and strategies to help her deal with me and to also educate herself more on my diagnosis. She has been instrumental in my recovery, taking care of me when I need it most. I can rely on her for anything and everything, and I don't know what I would do without her.

One of the most powerful contributors to a person recovering from BPD success is their support group around them. I have been blessed with amazing friends and family, who are so supportive of me, especially during my trying times. I can only imagine the frustration of someone having to deal with someone with BPD, because

I know how unstable we can be. Without my friends and family, I would not have the strength in me that I do today, and I would not have progressed as quickly to the better place I'm currently in. They are my reason to smile each day and stick with this PMA (positive mental attitude). Each day is tough, but I know that there is hope in living with and finding balance and peace within the clutches of BPD.

Currently, getting out of bed is still a daily struggle. I set my alarm for 6:00 a.m. and take my medication, and then give myself another hour in bed, to allow it to kick in. I have to push myself out of bed, knowing I have to face whatever the day may bring. It would be so easy for me to stay in bed all day, isolating myself and not facing anyone, or anything. I'd prefer it, actually. But that is not how we make progress towards our recovery. Each tiny step forward, is a huge feat for us. Each positive word we say to ourselves is pushing us forward, towards our recovery. Some days are particularly hard, while others are pretty good. I'm slowly getting back to that happy place, and I can see a light at the end of the tunnel, one that is growing brighter with each passing day. We can all get there; there is hope for all of us struggling with BPD.

Who makes up your support system?

My advice to those who are dealing with BPD directly or indirectly is to surround yourself with positive people who will support you no matter what. Have them learn about BPD and become familiar with its characteristics. Having them understand potential triggers is important because being able to recognize triggers may help you or them defuse the situation and symptoms, or it may help prevent a BPD episode from happening all together. But managing your triggers takes time and practice. It's important to stay mindful when you're in a triggered state and stay present in the moment. Not allowing those past or future thoughts affect your mood can feel like a daunting task. But the more we work on ourselves and practice being mindful, it makes managing our triggers that much easier. Sharing our stories, struggles, and making more people aware of BPD, depression, and anxiety is only the beginning of our road to recovery as a community. But it is a significant beginning.

Michelle McFatridge began BPD Connects (www.bpdconnects.com), a support group dedicated to those who suffer directly or indirectly from borderline personality disorder, anxiety and depression, to fill a much-needed gap for support groups and recovery tools. The BPD Connects mission is to assist those in whatever challenges they may be facing and identify coping strategies to aid in their road to recovery. Their goal is to raise awareness about BPD and mental illness, and remove the stigma associated with it.

Conclusion

The Importance of Self-Care

You may have noticed a similar thread in these stories: The importance of support. Support is vital for all healthy individuals, but is especially so for those going through trauma. And BPD is definitely a traumatic experience. It is traumatic for those who live with it every day, who are unable to regulate their emotions and reactions, and who have difficulty leading a life they want to live due to their body and brain reacting in ways they can't control. It's traumatic for loved ones who experience the whirlwind of emotions, sometimes becoming victims, and never knowing what to expect or how to interact with the person they love. They fear that they will be harmed, emotionally or physically, or that they will induce harm to their loved one by saying or doing the wrong thing. Finally, it can be a traumatic experience for therapists, who work hard to teach their patients strategies to avoid self-harm, and who often face the brunt of their patients' anger themselves. Therapists face disheartening defeat when their patients self-harm and attempt suicide, sometimes succeeding. They face waves of second-guessing themselves and treatment.

Whether you are the caregiver of an adolescent with BPD or the spouse of someone suffering from BPD, the emotional strain can be exhausting. In many ways, loved ones have to retrain how they respond and react. Many will feel constantly on guard and anxious. Caregivers will find, though, that if they are stressed or exhausted, they are less able to help their loved one in their recovery. Randi Kreger outlines five "power tools" for caretakers in her book *The Essential Family Guide to Borderline Personality Disorder*:

1. **Take good care of yourself.** Kreger stresses the importance of building a strong support system, including with those who do not have a relationship with your loved one struggling with BPD. Being part of a larger community, either through church or hobbies, is also encouraged. Taking deep breaths and the importance of sleep are highlighted, which seem to be common sense but are often overlooked.

2. **Uncover what keeps your feelings stuck.** Find a therapist who meets your needs. Your therapist will help you view your situation in a different light and teach you effective ways of communicating. Your therapist will help you learn to not personalize situations, and to instead work on problem-solving skills.

3. **Communicate to be heard.** Communication that is uplifting and helpful is key in establishing a safe environment, both for the person struggling with BPD and the caregiver. Kreger promotes talking, rather than yelling, explaining that people with BPD process information differently, and that it is an important thing to remember. She suggests taking three steps to build a stronger foundation for communicating: build groundwork, prepare to

communicate, and use intentional communication. When ready to communicate a particular issue, use her D.E.A.R. acronym: describe, express, assert, and reinforce.

4. **Set limits with love.** Boundaries can be difficult to set, and setting them can often result in behaviors becoming worse before they get better. However, setting boundaries is a way of *showing* love. They show you care not only about yourself but also about your relationship with your loved one with BPD. In setting boundaries, you must be prepared to enforce consequences of not following them. These limits allow those in the relationship to know what to expect and have some sort of control of the outcome.

5. **Reinforce the right behavior.** When setting boundaries, it is important to focus on *rewarding* experiences when the boundaries are followed. Rewarding following these boundaries at unexpected intervals is scientifically shown to increase the desired outcome and strengthen the positive behavior.

Self-care is important. For those with BPD, actively seeking treatment is a form of self-care. For therapists, a highly encouraged and integrated part of the DBT process is going to a support group for therapists treating those with BPD. This is suggested for any therapists treating BPD, whether they are using DBT as a form of therapy or not. It is essential to decompress, vent, and get outside perspective on their reactions and feelings while treating difficult cases. For family and loved ones, the preceding self-care guidance is a great way to ward off the issues related to burnout, resentment, and fatigue.

While all of these stories are different, you'll find a good support system was crucial to the recovery process. A support system can be many different things: face-to-face relationships, therapy teams, personal lasting friendships you can rely on, et cetera. With that in mind, the following section includes resources and links to expand your support system. Blogs from those suffering with BPD will help you feel less alone. Online chat groups can help you identify those who are where you are or have been where you are; these individuals can offer insight and resources specific to your needs. You'll also find therapy options, whether it's help in finding a therapist near you, virtual therapy, or even self-therapy. You'll find other resources as well, from smart phone applications, to books from experts in the field and those who have lived through a similar experience.

Thank you for your dedication to recovery, whether it's for yourself or if it is to help another live and recover through this experience. Recovery isn't easy. But it's worth it.

Resources

Resources are included based on peer-reviewed helpfulness and utility. No profit or other benefits were offered to the author, editors, writers, or publisher to include the following information.

Apps

DBT Diary Card

By Dr. Sammy Banawan, Durham DBT, Inc., and Therapy Apps, LLC

This app allows users to enter and track progress as they continue to practice DBT therapy skills outside the therapy office and in the real world. The app lets users enter information for the current day or previous days, visit the DBT coaching section for tips, customize the skills section, and maintain their privacy with the app's privacy lock.

Diarycard.net | Available on iTunes

DBT Selfhelp and Diary Card
By Cognitus Psychotherapy and Development
DBT Selfhelp lets users practice skills, track results, and monitor their mood and behavior. This new app includes diary cards and lets the user share them. It is highly recommended for both patients and professionals.
Dbt-app.com | Available on iTunes and Google Play

Headspace
The Headspace app guides users through meditation and helps them regularly practice mindfulness. It teaches the user how to meditate, journal, and use the buddy system.
Headspace.com | Available on iTunes, Google Play, and Amazon

NAMI AIR
National Alliance of Mental Illness (NAMI) AIR is a safe, anonymous social app to share and air your experiences. AIR (Anonymous. Inspiring. Relatable.) is a free, mobile-based social network designed for individuals living with mental health conditions and their family members/caregivers.
Nami.org | Available on iTunes and Google Play

Optimism
These self-tracking applications are designed to help users increase their understanding of all the things that can affect mental health. The apps act as a springboard to detect health patterns and develop strategies to proactively manage mental health conditions. This top-rated app also has a section for clinicians.
Findingoptimism.com | Available on iTunes, for Windows and Mac, and as a browser-based online application

Safety Net

This app is easily found by its distinctive green plus sign. This free app, designed by Two Penguin Studios, lets users develop a safety plan to be used when they feel distressed or approaching a suicidal crisis. Create and share your safety plan with clinicians and loved ones. The app provides GPS location services and contacts for professionals and agencies that can help.

By Two Penguin Studios LLC | Available on iTunes and Google Play

Suicide Safe

Designed for primary care and behavioral health providers, this app is a suicide-prevention learning tool based on the nationally recognized Suicide Assessment Five-step Evaluation and Triage (SAFE-T) practice guidelines. It offers providers tips on effective communication with patients and their families, guidance for working with patients who present with suicidal ideation, and referrals to treatment and community resources.

By SAMHSA | Available on iTunes and Google Play

Blogs

Borderline Personality Treatment

borderlinepersonalitytreatment.com
This informational blog was created for people affected by BPD. Treatment staff members from the Clearview Women's Center in Los Angeles, a BPD treatment facility for women, share their expertise, providing readers with details about BPD symptoms, co-occurring disorders, and treatment options.

BPD Transformation

bpdtransformation.wordpress.com

Edward Dantes' blog offers a male perspective on what it is like to have BPD and outlines his path to recovery from BPD symptoms.

The Fight within Us: Rethink BPD

thefightwithinus.com

Blogger Amanda Wang shares her "quest to find meaning in suffering." Through her blog and speaking engagements, she shares her own story—the struggles, setbacks, and breakthroughs—to give others the courage to endure.

Healing from BPD

my-borderline-personality-disorder.com

This blog offers resources and information for those suffering from BPD, including a chat room and links to published works.

My Borderline Mind

myborderlinemind.wordpress.com

This blog offers a thorough inside look from someone with BPD. In addition to discussing co-occurring illnesses, treatments, symptoms, and coping methods, it shares BPD portrayed in the media, quotes about BPD, and public figures with the disorder.

Books

The books listed here present a comprehensive reading list for patients, loved ones, and professionals dealing with BPD.

ADVANCED READING

These books, intended for mental health professionals, contain technical and psychological terminology. Nonprofessionals may still find the material contains pertinent information not available in other books.

Bateman, Anthony, MA, FRC Psych, and Peter Fonagy, PhD, FBA. *Handbook of Mentalizing in Mental Health Practice.* Washington, DC: American Psychiatric Publishing, 2012.

Bateman, Anthony, MA, FRC, and Peter Fonagy, PhD, FBA. *Psychotherapy for Borderline Personality Disorder: Mentalization-Based Treatment.* Oxford: Oxford University Press, 2004.

Bleiberg, Efrain, MD. *Treating Personality Disorders in Children and Adolescents: A Relational Approach.* New York: Guilford Press, 2004.

Diagnostic and Statistical Manual of Mental Disorders: DSM-5. Washington, DC: American Psychiatric Association, 2013.

Dimeff, Linda A., and Kelly Koerner. *Dialectical Behavior Therapy in Clinical Practice: Applications across Disorders and Settings.* New York: Guilford Press, 2007.

Foa, Edna, and Elizabeth Hembree. *Prolonged Exposure Therapy for PTSD: Emotional Processing of Traumatic Experiences.* Oxford: Oxford University Press, 2007.

Frankl, Viktor, and Alexander Batthyany. *The Feelings of Meaninglessness: A Challenge to Psychotherapy and Philosophy.* Milwaukee, WI: Marquette University Press, 2010.

Gunderson, John G., MD, and Paul S. Links. *Borderline Personality Disorder: A Clinical Guide.* Washington, DC: American Psychiatric Publishing, 2008.

Gunderson, John G., MD, and Perry D. Hoffman. *Understanding and Treating Borderline Personality Disorder: A Guide for Professionals and Families.* Washington, DC: American Psychiatric Publishing, 2005.

Hoffman, Perry D., PhD, and Penny Steiner-Grossman, EdD, MPH. *Borderline Personality Disorder: Meeting the Challenges to Successful Treatment.* Binghamton, NY: Haworth Press, 2007.

Judd, Patricia Hoffman, and Thomas H. McGlashan. *A Developmental Model of Borderline Personality Disorder: Understanding Variations in Course and Outcome.* Washington, DC: American Psychiatric Publishing, 2003

Koerner, Kelly. *Doing Dialectical Behavior Therapy: A Practical Guide.* New York: Guilford Press, 2012.

Leahy, Robert, Dennis Tirch, and Lisa Napolitano. *Emotion Regulation in Psychotherapy: A Practitioner's Guide.* New York: Guilford Press, 2011.

Linehan, Marsha, PhD. *Skills Training Manual for Treating Borderline Personality Disorder.* New York: Guilford Press, 1993.

Paris, Joel, MD. *Treatment of Borderline Personality Disorder: A Guide to Evidence-Based Practice.* New York: Guilford Press, 2008.

Practice Guideline for the Treatment of Patients with Borderline Personality Disorder. Washington, DC: American Psychiatric Association, 2001.

Preston, John, PsyD. *Integrative Treatment for Borderline Personality Disorder: Effective, Symptom-Focused Techniques, Simplified for Private Practice.* Oakland, CA: New Harbinger Publications, 2006.

Zvolensky, Michael, Amit Bernstein, and Anka Vujanovic. *Distress Tolerance: Theory, Research, and Clinical Application.* New York: Guilford Press, 2010.

MEMOIRS

These books contain stories that may be triggering to readers with BPD, but offer great insight and hope. They are encouraged reading for all those affected or touched by BPD in their lives.

Blauner, Susan Rose. *How I Stayed Alive when My Brain Was Trying to Kill Me: One Person's Guide to Suicide Prevention.* New York: Quill, 2003.

Coffey, Helen Cochran. *Don't Let Anyone Know: A Story about Mental Illness—the World Viewed Only the Silhouette!* Bloomington, IN: Xlibris Corporation, 2012.

Corso, Debbie. *Healing from Borderline Personality Disorder: My Journey out of Hell through Dialectical Behavior Therapy.* Amazon, 2012.

Fitzpatrick, David. *Sharp: My Story of Madness, Cutting, and How I Reclaimed My Life.* New York: William Morrow, 2013.

Gelder, Kiera Van. *The Buddha and the Borderline: My Recovery from Borderline Personality Disorder through Dialectical Behavior Therapy, Buddhism, and Online Dating.* Oakland, CA: New Harbinger Publications, 2010.

Johnson, Merri Lisa. *Girl in Need of a Tourniquet: Memoir of a Borderline Personality.* Berkeley, CA: Seal Press, 2010.

Pershall, Stacy. *Loud in the House of Myself: Memoir of a Strange Girl.*
New York: W. W. Norton, 2011.

Reiland, Rachel. *Get Me out of Here: My Recovery from Borderline
Personality Disorder.* Center City, MN: Hazelden, 2004.

Tusiani, Bea, and Paula Tusiani-Eng. *Remnants of a Life on Paper:
A Mother and Daughter's Struggle with Borderline Personality Disorder.*
New York: Baroque Press, 2013.

SKILLS AND TOOLS
*These books are intended for those struggling with BPD and looking for
management tools and techniques.*

Anderson, Susan. *The Journey from Abandonment to Healing.* New York:
Berkley Publishing Group, 2000.

Aron, Elaine N. *The Highly Sensitive Person: How to Thrive When the World
Overwhelms You.* New York: Broadway Books, 1997.

Beck, Aaron T. *Prisoners of Hate: The Cognitive Basis of Anger, Hostility,
and Violence.* New York: Harper Perennial, 2000.

Bockian, Neil R., Valerie Porr, and Nora Elizabeth Villagran. *New Hope for
People with Borderline Personality Disorder.* Roseville, CA: Prima, 2002.

Brown, C. Brené. *I Thought It Was Just Me (But It Isn't): Telling the Truth
about Perfectionism, Inadequacy, and Power.* New York: Gotham, 2008.

Burns, David D., MD. *The Feeling Good Handbook.* New York:
Plume, 1999.

Chapman, Alexander L., PhD, and Kim L. Gratz. *Borderline Personality
Disorder: A Guide for the Newly Diagnosed.* Oakland, CA: New
Harbinger Publications, 2013.

Chapman, Alexander L., PhD, and Kim L. Gratz. *The Borderline Personality Disorder Survival Guide: Everything You Need to Know about Living with BPD.* Oakland, CA: New Harbinger Publications, 2007.

Friedel, Robert O., MD. *Borderline Personality Disorder Demystified: An Essential Guide for Understanding and Living with BPD.* New York: Da Capo Press, 2004.

Goleman, Daniel. *Destructive Emotions: How Can We Overcome Them? A Scientific Dialogue with the Dalai Lama.* New York: Bantam, 2003.

Goleman, Daniel. *Emotional Intelligence.* New York: Bantam, 1995.

Goleman, Daniel. *Healing Emotions: Conversations with the Dalai Lama on Mindfulness, Emotions, and Health.* Boston: Shambhala, 1997.

Gottman, John Mordechai, and Joan DeClaire. *The Relationship Cure: A Five-Step Guide to Strengthening Your Marriage, Family, and Friendships.* New York: Three Rivers, 2002.

Gratz, Kim, and Alexander Chapman. *Freedom from Self-Harm: Overcoming Self-Injury with Skills from DBT and Other Treatments.* Oakland, CA: New Harbinger Publications, 2009.

Green, Tami. *Self-Help for Managing the Symptoms of Borderline Personality Disorder.* Houston, TX: T. Green, 2008.

Kreger, Randi, and Erik Gunn. *The ABC's of BPD: The Basics of Borderline Personality Disorder.* Milwaukee, WI: Eggshells, 2007.

Kreisman, Jerold J., MD, and Hal Straus. *Sometimes I Act Crazy: Living with Borderline Personality Disorder.* Hoboken, NJ: John Wiley & Sons, 2004.

Mondimore, Francis Mark, MD, and Patrick Kelly, MD. *Borderline Personality Disorder: New Reasons for Hope*. Baltimore: Johns Hopkins University Press, 2011.

Moskovitz, MD., Richard A. *Lost in the Mirror: An Inside Look at Borderline Personality Disorder*. Dallas, TX: Taylor Trade Publishing, 2001.

Oldham, John M., MD, and Lois B. Morris. *The New Personality Self-Portrait: Why You Think, Work, Love, and Act the Way You Do*. New York: Bantam, 1995.

DBT AND MINDFULNESS

Aguirre, Blaise A., and Gillian Galen, PsyD. *Mindfulness for Borderline Personality Disorder: Relieve Your Suffering Using the Core Skill of Dialectical Behavior Therapy*. Oakland, CA: New Harbinger Publications, 2013.

Albers, Susan. *Eating Mindfully: How to End Mindless Eating and Enjoy a Balanced Relationship with Food*. Oakland, CA: New Harbinger Publications, 2003.

Brantley, Jeffrey. *Calming Your Anxious Mind: How Mindfulness and Compassion Can Free You from Anxiety, Fear, and Panic*. 2nd ed. Oakland, CA: New Harbinger Publications, 2007.

Brantley, Jeffrey, and Wendy Millstine. *True Belonging: Mindful Practices to Help You Overcome Loneliness, Connect with Others, and Cultivate Happiness*. Oakland, CA: New Harbinger Publications, 2011.

Corso, Debbie. *Stop Sabotaging: A 31-Day DBT Challenge to Change Your Life*. Amazon, 2013.

Kabat-Zinn, Jon, and Thich Nhat Hanh. *Full Catastrophe Living: Using the Wisdom of Your Body and Mind to Face Stress, Pain, and Illness.* New York, New York: Bantam, 2003 (Revised Edition).

Kumar, Sameet. *Grieving Mindfully: A Compassionate and Spiritual Guide to Coping with Loss.* Oakland, CA: New Harbinger Publications, 2005.

Linehan, Marsha. *DBT Skills Training Handouts and Worksheets.* 2nd ed. New York: Guilford Press, 2014.

McKay, Matthew, PhD, Jeffrey C. Wood, PhD, and Jeffrey Brantley, MD. *The Dialectical Behavior Therapy Skills Workbook: Practical DBT Exercises for Learning Mindfulness, Interpersonal Effectiveness, Emotion Regulation, and Distress Tolerance.* Oakland, CA: New Harbinger Publications, 2007.

Smith, Amanda. *The Dialectical Behavior Therapy Wellness Planner: 365 Days of Healthy Living for Your Body, Mind, and Spirit.* Scottsdale, AZ: Unhooked Books, 2015.

Spradlin, Scott E. *Don't Let Your Emotions Run Your Life: How Dialectical Behavior Therapy Can Put You in Control.* Oakland, CA: New Harbinger Publications, 2003.

FOR LOVED ONES

What follows is a list of incredible books that have been peer reviewed and are highly effective, whether you're a parent, significant other, sibling, child, or other loved one in the life of someone struggling with BPD.

Aguirre, Blaise A. *Borderline Personality Disorder in Adolescents: What to Do When Your Teen Has BPD.* Beverly, MA: Fair Winds, 2014

Fruzzetti, Alan. *The Family Guide to Borderline Personality Disorder; Finding Peace in Your Family Using Dialectical Behavior Therapy.* Oakland, CA: New Harbinger Publications, 2015.

Fruzzetti, Alan E., PhD. *The High-Conflict Couple: A Dialectical Behavior Therapy Guide to Finding Peace, Intimacy and Validation.* Oakland, CA: New Harbinger Publications, 2006.

Green, Tami. *Helping Someone You Love Recover from Borderline Personality Disorder (Finally and Completely).* Houston, TX: T. Green, 2008.

Hall, Karyn D., PhD, Melissa H. Cook, LPC, and Shari Y. Manning, PhD. *The Power of Validation: Arming Your Child Against Bullying, Peer Pressure, Addiction, Self-Harm and Out-of-Control Emotions.* Oakland, CA: New Harbinger Publications, 2012.

Harvey, Pat, ACSW LCSW-C, and Jeanine A. Penzo, LICSW. *Parenting a Child Who Has Intense Emotions: Dialectical Behavior Therapy Skills to Help Your Child Regulate Emotional Outbursts and Aggressive Behaviors.* Oakland, CA: New Harbinger Publications, 2009.

Kaplan, Cynthia, PhD, Blaise A. Aguirre, MD, and Michael Rater, MD. *Helping Your Troubled Teen: Learn to Recognize, Understand, and Address the Destructive Behavior of Today's Teens.* Beverly, MA: Fair Winds, 2007.

Karp, Harvey, and Paula Spencer. *The Happiest Toddler on the Block: How to Eliminate Tantrums and Raise a Patient, Respectful, and Cooperative One- to Four-Year-Old.* New York: Bantam, 2008.

Khemlani-Patel, Sony, Merry McVey-Noble, and Fugen Neziroglu. *When Your Child Is Cutting: A Parent's Guide to Helping Children Overcome Self-Injury.* Oakland, CA: New Harbinger Publications, 2006.

Komrad, Mark S., MD. *You Need Help! A Step-by-Step Plan to Convince a Loved One to Get Counseling.* Center City, MN: Hazelden, 2012.

Krawitz, Roy, and Wendy Jackson. *Borderline Personality Disorder.* Oxford, UK: Oxford University Press, 2008.

Kreger, Randi. *The Essential Family Guide to Borderline Personality Disorder: New Tools and Techniques to Stop Walking on Eggshells.* Center City, MN: Hazelden, 2008.

Lawson, Christine Ann, PhD. *Understanding the Borderline Mother: Helping Her Children Transcend the Intense, Unpredictable and Volatile Relationship.* Lanham, MD: Rowman & Littlefield Publishers, 2000.

Lundberg, Gary B., and Joy Saunders Lundberg. *I Don't Have to Make Everything All Better: Six Practical Principles to Empower Others to Solve Their Own Problems While Enriching Your Relationships.* New York: Penguin, 2000.

Manning, Shari Y., PhD. *Loving Someone with Borderline Personality Disorder: How to Keep Out-of-Control Emotions from Destroying Your Relationship.* New York: Guilford Press, 2011.

Mason, Paul T., MS, and Randi Kreger. *Stop Walking on Eggshells: Taking Your Life Back When Someone You Care about Has Borderline Personality Disorder.* Oakland, CA: New Harbinger Publications, 2010.

Porr, Valerie. *Overcoming Borderline Personality Disorder: A Family Guide for Healing and Change.* Oxford, UK: Oxford University Press, 2010.

Roth, Kimberlee, and Freda B. Friedman, PhD, LDSW. *Surviving a Borderline Parent: How to Heal Your Childhood Wounds and Build Trust, Boundaries, and Self-Esteem.* Oakland, CA: New Harbinger Publications, 2003.

Winkler, K., and Randi Kreger. *Hope for Parents: Helping Your Borderline Son or Daughter without Sacrificing Your Family or Yourself.* Milwaukee, WI: Eggshells Press, 2000.

Foundations

These organizations work to bring awareness of BPD, to increase availability of therapy options, and to reach those touched by this disorder.

Brain & Behavior Research Foundation

bbrfoundation.org/bpd

The BBR Foundation is "committed to alleviating the suffering caused by mental illness by awarding grants that will lead to advances and breakthroughs in scientific research."

Families for Borderline Personality Disorder (BPD) Research

familiesforbpdresearch.org

This organization is comprised of "a grassroots group of family members, friends, and others who have loved ones living with BPD," committed to supporting BPD research.

National Alliance on Mental Illness (NAMI)

nami.org

NAMI offers various face-to-face free support groups to help not only those who suffer from mental illness but loved ones as well. You can search their site to find a location/meeting near you. You can also explore NAMI Peer-to-Peer, an education course open to anyone experiencing mental health challenges, and NAMI Provider Education, which offers a class for staff at mental health treatment facilities.

NEA-BPD: National Education Alliance for
Borderline Personality Disorder

borderlinepersonalitydisorder.com

The NEA-BPD "works with families and persons in recovery, raises public awareness, provides education to professionals, promotes research, and works with Congress to enhance the quality of life for those affected by this serious but treatable mental illness."

TARA: Treatment and Research Advancements
for Borderline Personality Disorder

tara4bpd.org

TARA sponsors an eight-session DBT family training workshop in cities across the country. Each training cycle is limited to 16 members, and a registration fee is required. Founder and author Valerie Porr is an active supporter of raising awareness of BPD.

Online Support

These sites contain forums, therapy options, and useful information.

BPD Family

bpdfamily.com

The collective work of 75,000 members and over 3 million articles and posts, BPD Family is a resource for the family members of those affected by BPD to have a strong support system outside the home. It is a "safe place for intelligent discussion and freedom from the egos and tempers that plague many large blogs and message boards."

BPD Recovery

bpdrecovery.com

This site focuses on self-help recovering from BPD using tools that are predominantly CBT oriented.

BPD World

bpdworld.org

This comprehensive site offers detailed information about BPD, as well as support groups and even online/distance counseling at very low fees. You can also take courses, watch educational videos, and find a therapist.

Cognitive Behavior Therapy Self-Help Resources

getselfhelp.co.uk/dbt.htm

This site offers a multitude of self-help opportunities.

DBT Path

emotionallysensitive.com

DBT Path offers online DBT Skills Training classes with sliding scale.

DBT Self Help

dbtselfhelp.com

This site offers ways to learn about and practice DBT each day.

Finding Balance

findingbalance.com

Many individuals with BPD struggle with self-harming behaviors as a means to cope with emotional reaction. This is a site for those who struggle in this area, offering weekly group and 24/7 peer support.

Regional Assistance

In many areas, there are no BPD-specific programs, but the following countries have a wide range of resources available. Find organizations in your country and region that promote awareness, fund research, and provide assistance to those affected by BPD.

AUSTRALIA

Australia BPD Foundation

bpdfoundation.org.au

The foundation promotes a positive culture to support the recovery journey of people with BPD and their families/caregivers. It also supports health care professionals working in the field.

SANE Australia

sane.org

This national charity serves all Australians affected by mental health illness.

CANADA

BPD Connects

bpdconnects.com

Located in Mississauga, Ontario, BPD Connects offers support groups for those who suffer from mental health illness, focusing on CBT and DBT methods.

Canada Mental Health Association

cmha.ca

The Canada Mental Health Association helps those with BPD find nearby support groups.

Hereto Help

heretohelp.bc.ca

A combined venture of seven agencies, Here to Help offers links to therapy services, self-screening, and general information.

FRANCE

AAPEL

aapel.org

This site, aimed at those with BPD, offers help and support.

UNITED KINGDOM

The British and Irish Group for the Study of Personality Disorder

bigspd.org.uk

This comprehensive site contains extensive information about BPD, offers connections for support groups, and shares resources for online/ distance counseling with low fees.

The Consortium for Therapeutic Communities

therapeuticcommunities.org

The consortium links people with mental health issues to therapeutic communities and environments. Visit the site to learn more about therapeutic communities and find one close to you.

Emergence

emergenceplus.org.uk

This site is made by patients, for patients. It was formerly known as Borderline UK and is a great starting place if you think you may have BPD.

Health in Mind

health-in-mind.org.uk

Health in Mind offers a Scotland-wide counseling telephone line. Visit their Information Resource Center for information relating to mental health and well-being.

Kathi's Mental Health Review

toddlertime.com

This site was designed as a foundation and cutting-edge source for BPD for consumers, students, and professionals.

NHS Choice

nhs.uk

This site helps those with BPD find local resources, support, programs, and therapists.

USA

BPD Global

bpdglobal.com

This nonprofit organization teaches BPD Survival Skills classes.

Clearview Women's Center

clearviewwomenscenter.com

A premier provider of BPD treatment, the Clearview Women's Center in Los Angeles has a staff of extensively trained dialectical behavior therapy (DBT) therapists.

Florida Borderline Personality Disorder Association

fbpda.org

This association offers information and resources for those suffering from BPD, as well as friends and loved ones of those with BPD.

McLean Hospital's Center for the Treatment of Borderline Personality Disorder

mclean.harvard.edu/patient/adult/bpd.php

This small supportive residential community helps women coping with BPD or other complex disorders by providing "the tools and guidance needed to foster the self-reliance needed to build a balanced and more effective life."

Mental Health America

mentalhealthamerica.net

Mental Health America is the nation's leading community-based nonprofit, dedicated to helping all Americans achieve wellness by living mentally healthier lives. It offers services to locate local resources and therapy.

New England Personality Disorder Association (NEPDA)

nepda.org

This association offers BPD family workshops, regional conferences, education, advocacy, and support.

Roanne Program

roanneprogram.com

The coed Roanne Program is the only program specializing in BPD for people aged between 17 and 28.

Center for Mindfulness Stress-Reduction Program at University of Massachusetts Medical School

umassmed.edu/cfm/stress-reduction

The center offers workshops on mindfulness throughout the country, as well as local and online resources.

Informative/Helpful Websites and Other Resources

The following websites offer a multitude of benefits, from in-depth information about BPD to articles, documentaries, podcasts, and other resources.

About Anything to Stop the Pain

anythingtostopthepain.com

This site is for partners and parents of people with BPD.

Back from the Edge

youtu.be/967Ckat7f98

This video offers guidance on treating BPD, created by the Borderline Personality Disorder Resource Center at New York–Presbyterian Hospital.

Behavioral Tech

behavioraltech.com

This site will help you find a DBT therapist or professional training and resources.

BPD Awareness Page

bpdawareness.org or Facebook.com/bpda1

This site offers easy access resources, reviews, article sharing, and community talk.

BPD Central

bpdcentral.com

BPD Central is one of the longest-established, most popular, and largest sites about BPD. Here you will find a support group, resources, information, and a community support group in the thousands.

Borderline Personality Disorder Demystified

bpddemystified.com

Robert O. Friedel, MD, wrote the book by the same name and keeps comprehensive resources and news about BPD on his site. Here you can take a self-test for BPD and find in-depth information about the disorder.

Borderline Personality Disorder from the Inside Out

borderlinepersonality.ca

This site offers BPD information, support, ebooks, audio, videos, the *BPD Inside Out* podcast, over a decade worth of articles, and nearly 300 posts.

Borderline Personality Disorder Resource Center

bpdresourcecenter.org

The Borderline Personality Disorder Resource Center was established to help those affected by BPD "find the most current and accurate information on the nature of BPD, and on sources of available treatment." Professional resources are available as well.

Brandon Marshall's Project Borderline

projectborderline.org

A professional football player and activist's site to raise awareness for BPD.

Hope for BPD

hopeforbpd.com

Treatment navigation and support for BPD and self-injury by Amanda Smith, the founder of the Florida BPD Association. Offers webinars and other helpful information.

If Only We Had Known: A Family Guide to
Borderline Personality Disorder

bpdvideo.com

Bpdvideo.com offers support, connection, and resources to those with BPD.

My Dialectical Life

mydialecticallife.com

This peer-led email service was designed to help individuals who are currently working with a licensed therapist or mental health professional get an extra boost in their DBT Skills Training, and to stay connected with what they've already learned.

Personality Lab

personalitylab.org

This site offers free personality feedback using tests developed by research psychologists at University of California, Berkeley.

References

American Psychiatric Association. *Diagnostic and Statistical Manual of Mental Disorders,* 4th ed., text rev. Washington, DC: American Psychiatric Association, 2000.

American Psychiatric Association. *Diagnostic and Statistical Manual of Mental Disorders,* 5th ed. Washington, DC: American Psychiatric Association, 2013.

Beck, A. T., ed., Denise Davis, ed., and Arthur Freeman, ed. *Cognitive Therapy of Personality Disorders,* 3rd ed. New York: Guilford Press, 2014.

Bertsch, Katja, Ilinca Schmidinger, Inga Neuman, and Sabine Herpertz. "Reduced Plasma Oxytocin Levels in Female Patients with Borderline Personality Disorder." *Hormones and Behavior* 63, no. 3 (2013): 424–29. doi: 10.1016/j.yhbeh.2012.11.013.

Binks, Claire, Mark Fenton, Lucy McCarthy, Tracy Lee, Clive E. Adams, and Conor Duggan, "Pharmacological Interventions for People with Borderline Personality Disorder." *Cochrane Developmental, Psychosocial, and Learning Problems Group* (January 2006). doi: 10.1002/14651858.CD005653.

Brunner, Jose, and Orna Ophir. "In Good Times and in Bad: Boundary Relations of Psychoanalysis in Post-War USA." *History of Psychiatry* 22, no. 2 (June 2011): 215–231. doi: 10.1177/0957154X11401182.

Dingfelder, Sadie. "Treatment for the 'Untreatable'." *Monitor on Psychology* 35, no. 3 (March 2004): 46. http://www.apa.org/monitor/mar04/treatment.aspx.

Friedel, Robert. *Borderline Personality Disorder Demystified*. New York: Marlowe & Company, 2004.

Hankin, Benjamin, Andrea L. Barrocas, Jessica Jenness, Caroline W. Oppenheimer, Lisa S. Badanes, John R. Z. Abela, Jami Young, and Andrew Smolen. "Association Between 5-HTTLPR and Borderline Personality Disorder Traits Among Youth." *Frontiers in Psychiatry* 2, no. 6 (March 2011): 1–7. doi: 10.3389/fpsyt.2011.00006.

Kreger, Randi. *The Essential Family Guide to Borderline Personality Disorder*. Minnesota: Hazeldon, 2008.

Leichsenring, Falk, and Eric Leibing. "The Effectiveness of Psychodynamic Therapy and Cognitive Behavior Therapy in the Treatment of Personality Disorders: A Meta-Analysis." *American Journal of Psychiatry* 160, no. 7 (July 2003): 1223–32. doi: 10.1176/appi.ajp.160.7.1223.

Linehan, Marsha. "The Empirical Basis of Dialectical Behavior Therapy: Development of New Treatments versus Evaluation of Existing Treatments." *Clinical Psychology: Science and Practice* 7, no. 1 (March 2000): 113–19. doi: 10.1093/clipsy.7.1.113.

Millon, Theodore. *Disorders of Personality: DSM-IV and Beyond*, 2nd ed. New York: Wiley, 1995.

Searles, Harold. *My Work with Borderline Patients*. Northvale, NJ: Aronson, 1986.

Searles, Harold. "Phases of Patient-Therapist Interaction in the Psychotherapy of Chronic Schizophrenia." *British Journal of Medical Psychology* 34, no 3–4 (December 1961): 169ologydoi: 10.1111/j.2044-8341.1961.tb00944.x.

Stanley, Barbara, and Larry Siever. "The Interpersonal Dimension of Borderline Personality Disorder: Toward a Neuropeptide Model." *The American Journal of Psychiatry* 167, no. 1 (January 2010): 24–39. doi: 10.1176/appi.ajp.2009.09050744.

Stern, Adolf. "Psychoanalytic Investigation of and Therapy in the Border Line Group of Neuroses." *The Psychoanalytic Quarterly* 7, (April 1938): 467–89.

Walter, Marc, Jean-François Bureau, Bjarne M. Holmes, Eszter A. Bertha, Michael Hollander, Joan Wheelis, Nancy Hall Brooks, and Karlen Lyons-Ruth. "Cortisol Response to Interpersonal Stress in Young Adults with Borderline Personality Disorder: A Pilot Study." *European Psychiatry: The Journal of the Association of European Psychiatrists* 23, no 3 (April 2008): 201–04. doi: 10.1016/j.curpsy.2007.12.003.

Zanarini, Mary, and Frances Frankenburg. "Omega-3 Fatty Acid Treatment of Women with Borderline Personality Disorder: A Double-Blind, Placebo-Controlled Pilot Study." *The American Journal of Psychiatry* 160, no 1 (January 2003):167iatrdoi: 10.1176/appi .ajp.160.1.167.

Index

U
unpredictability, 24
US Food and Drug Administration, 29

V
validation, 30

W
women, reducing aggression in, 30

Y
Young, Jeffrey, 29

About the Editor & Foreword Author

TABETHA MARTIN was introduced to the struggles of those with BPD when she was given custody of her adolescent sister who had been diagnosed with the disorder. While working toward her bachelor's degree in psychology at California State University, San Marcos, her life experiences with the disorder helped her specialize in the field. Her first paper on the subject was a psychoanalysis of Rachel Reiland, the author of one of the first BPD books Tabetha ever read. This paper went on to win Outstanding Psychology Paper for the 2011–2012 academic year. From there she worked on a parent's guideline pamphlet for newly diagnosed families and began running the Borderline Personality Disorder Awareness Page—a site that reaches tens of thousands of individuals each day. Currently, she is working toward her MSW and opening her own full-service mental health program for women (not just women with BPD).

PAULA TUSIANI-ENG lives in Garden City, New York, and is a mother to four children. Paula is currently promoting *Remnants of a Life on Paper*, a book she coauthored with her mother about her family. She is a writer and advocate for BPD and serves on the Board of the Borderline Personality Disorder Resource Center at New York–Presbyterian Hospital. Her goal is to raise awareness for this disorder.

Paula received her master's degree in divinity from Union Theological Seminary in New York in 2001. She worked as a pastoral associate for youth and families at Church of St. Anne in Garden City, New York. She also worked in the Office of Campus Ministry at Fordham University in the Bronx. She completed her master's degree in social work at Adelphi University in 2014.

Paula is a co-founder of Emotions Matter, Inc., a network of individuals, family members and communities impacted by Borderline Personality Disorder (BPD) that shares a mission to raise awareness of BPD and advocate for better mental healthcare. Visit Emotions Matter online at emotionsmatterbpd.org.

Acknowledgments

With no way to fully put my gratitude into words, I'd like to thank Timothy Martin. He was there when our journey into BPD began. He agreed without hesitation to our taking custody of my young sister, and he stumbled with me through the darkness of ignorance around how to help her. He held me many nights while I sobbed, not knowing how to help my sister, devastated at the pain she was going through. Years later, he sat with me and helped sort through submitted stories, where being able to identify and feel what the writers had gone through often left me in tears. Our pillar of support in keeping our home running and functional was and is our nanny, Beverly Breen, who has been through all of the struggles right alongside us.

Two of my professors left an impact on me, ensuring that what I was going through would be helpful to others in the future. Dr. Catherine Cucinella, PhD, director of the General Education Writing Program at CSUSM, encouraged me to use my writing abilities and words to reach others. Her kind words and constructive criticism left an enduring impression. Dr. Miriam Schustack, PhD, Psychology Chair for CSUSM, as well as writer and researcher, not only listened to my inquiry regarding borderline personality disorder, but also encouraged me through my exhaustion and frustration. She delved into my writings and musings on BPD, encouraging the submission of my work. Her expertise in the field of personality psychology was a great support and comfort to me during a time when I felt helpless.

Authors Dr. Blaise Aguirre, MD, and Randi Kreger were the cornerstone of support in our life in finding the best ways to deal with the struggles my sister was going through. With the rare chance of my sister's being diagnosed and treated as an adolescent, we faced both the benefits of knowing about her diagnosis and the downfall of the stigma attached to it. It was only after finally coming into contact with their books that we were able to change our family structure and interaction. You'll find a few contributors to this book will say the same.

These experiences led to my taking over administration of the Borderline Personality Awareness Page, bpdawareness.org, a page whose goals are to raise awareness, encourage conversation, share resources, and fight stigma. This book encompasses all of these goals.

While a project of this type has long been in my heart, it wasn't until my managing editor at Callisto Media, Nana Twumasi, approached me with similar hopes that it came to fruition. Nana was a positive force in helping to shape the manuscript, as we played with what worked best.

Thank you to Paula Tusiani-Eng, a kindred spirit and activist for those struggling with BPD, for her encouragement and input in this project.

Thank you all for your lasting encouragement, support, and guidance.

Printed in the USA
CPSIA information can be obtained
at www.ICGtesting.com
CBHW041526260324
5882CB00005B/16